PRAISE FOR
Soul Reset

We all long to be honest, genuine, and faithful people. With refreshing honesty, Dotson skillfully and vulnerably points us in the right direction. This book really spoke to me. It will speak to you too.

—ADAM HAMILTON
Author of *The Walk: Five Essential Practices of the Christian Life*

Junius Dotson is an amazing man of God. I love the heart that he has for God's people all over the world. Jesus told us to go into all the world and make disciples. Junius is spending his life giving everything he has to all those who will listen and learn how to make disciples for the cause of Christ. I pray that healing will come to many through Junius's journey to wholeness.

—CECE WINANS
GRAMMY Award®-winning gospel artist

True leaders aren't perfect; they're transparent. Junius's personal story compels us to be open about our struggles as we build mighty organizations full of people who can make a difference in this world. This book may change the way you lead.

—HANNAH PARAMORE BREEN
Founder, Paramore Digital
Nashville, TN

Every leader and every believer needs a copy of *Soul Reset*. It's the type of book that needs to be an annual read to help us realign our hearts for life and ministry. In the fast-paced culture of today, this book provides a fresh reminder of what's most important.

—BRYAN CARTER
Senior Pastor, Concord Church
Dallas, TX

This is not just another book on church leadership or discipleship. Junius Dotson's courageous, honest storytelling approach will make you look at your own life and find hope for what is ahead. That's what it did for me. You need to read this book!

—Jacob Armstrong
Pastor, Providence United Methodist Church
Mt. Juliet, TN

Hitting the reset button may be exactly what our souls need, but it's a scary step to take. Fortunately, Junius Dotson has already been down that path, and he invites us to take the journey in a way that is authentic and inspiring.

—Mike Bonem
Consultant, coach, and author of
Thriving in the Second Chair

Junius Dotson invites me—invites you—to be vulnerable by "being vulnerable." He confirms, through his own personal journey, that it is only when the emotional level is engaged that spiritual growth, personal growth, or "reset" have a chance. He provides a great process for each of us, especially through a small group—an emotional-spiritual walk worth taking.

—Rev. Bill Selby
President/Center Mentor, Center for
Pastoral Effectiveness of the Rockies
Highlands Ranch, CO

S○UL
RESET

breakdown, breakthrough,
and the journey to wholeness

JUNIUS B. DOTSON

UPPER
ROOM BOOKS®
NASHVILLE

Cover design: Tim Green, Faceout Studio
Cover imagery: Shutterstock
Typesetting and interior design: PerfecType | Nashville, TN

ISBNs
978-0-8358-1896-4 (print)
978-0-8358-1897-1 (mobi)
978-0-8358-1898-8 (ePub)

Printed in the United States of America

To those who refuse to give up on the dark days
and to the people in their lives who encourage them

CONTENTS

PREFACE

Reset is a word floating around in our culture today. We can reset our computers. We can reset our attitudes. We reset our relationships, our clocks, and our jewelry. But in recent years, a reset has taken on a deeper meaning. Making a reset can mean a rearranging of priorities, a reshaping of purpose and pursuit. Calling a reset means we're taking a time out, surveying the situation, and charting a new way forward. I love the image of the most impactful kind of reset—the factory reset. In a factory reset, you restore something all the way back to its beginning, clearing away clutter, old files and data, and starting fresh with a world of possibility before you. A factory reset is getting all the way back to the beginning and creating a new way forward.

I've taken the idea of a factory reset and applied it to my own soul. In this book, you'll read about my desperate need for a total and complete soul reset. I needed to get all the way back to the beginning settings in my heart, soul, and mind, to clear away clutter and old ways of doing things that were not only inefficient but also stealing my ability to function at my best. So, my definition of a *soul reset* is a hard stop of chronic busyness; a deep look inward and an intentional look to God; and a new, more holistic journey forward that more closely resembles an abundant life into which Jesus calls his disciples. A soul reset is the pouring out of one's self to God. It means laying yourself at the altar and earnestly seeking God's face. It means a season of fervent praying and fasting. It includes finding new and meaningful ways to connect with Jesus, the lover of our souls.

The ultimate goal of a soul reset is to live our best lives now. To experience the abundant life that Jesus promised us. Sometimes this means fighting for joy in the midst of difficult situations. The apostle Paul was in prison, getting ready to be executed, and he penned a letter to the church in Philippi about joy. He told them to "Always be joyful in the Lord, again, I say rejoice" (Phil. 4:4). It is not easy, but it is possible, especially when we remember that in God's presence is fullness of joy (see Psalm 16:11)!

In order to experience fullness of joy, part of our soul reset must include spiritual practices that help us stay close to God and order our lives in such a way that we avoid overcommitment, over-scheduling, and under-praying. Spiritual practices such as prayer, journaling, small groups, confession, and even lament keep us connected to God as we reset and reorder our lives in the path of abundance and joy versus busyness and being overwhelmed. Spiritual practices are so important and vital for our discipleship journey. They are not about being a better church member. They are not about being a perfect leader. They are not about having the appearance of religiosity or holiness. They are about growing in our relationship with God and staying in love with Jesus.

This is the foundation for healthy and whole living. It is the foundation for creating a healthy faith community. Each passing day teaches me that if I stay connected to Jesus and grounded in my faith, then no matter what problem I face, it doesn't have to overwhelm me. I am learning that no matter what I go through, I am not going through it alone. Remember,

> "When you pass through deep waters, I will be
> with you;
> your troubles will not overwhelm you.
> When you pass through fire, you will not be burned;
> the hard trials that come will not hurt you.
> For I am the LORD your God." (Isa. 43:2-3, GNT)

If you have lost your connection to the living God, I want to invite you to begin a soul reset. If you, like me, have found yourself too busy, too tired, too burned out on doing work for God, maybe you need a soul reset—a time to just be with God instead of doing things for God. If you are new to the Christian faith and have been searching for true joy and fullness of life, I want to invite you to do a soul reset and reorder your life around the love, grace, and goodness of God. If you are suffering anxiety or depression, are walking through a season of grief, or are stuck in a spirit of despair, I want to invite you to reset, to lean into the loving arms of God and know that you are so loved and you are not alone. Wherever you are on your journey toward God is the perfect place to begin.

My prayer is that your soul reset will set a new course for your life—maybe even lead you to breakthrough. A reset for me meant a new depth of joy and peace that I had never known. I still have trials, a ton of work to do, and a lurking anxiety and depression that tries to grab at me. But a reset gets me back to the beginning, and it helps me remember to stay connected to God through spiritual practices. I keep God first and keep enough margin in my days to breathe deeply, to listen to God, and to hear God remind me who I am. I believe that a soul reset will change the way you live, the way you lead yourself, and the way you lead others. As a result, your daily life, your family, your workplace, and your church will never be the same again.

In Jesus' name! Amen.

—Junius B. Dotson

ACKNOWLEDGMENTS

The emotional process of writing this book was much harder than I ever could have imagined. I want to say thank you to the incredible publishing team of The Upper Room for investing in the spiritual lives of leaders. I am most especially grateful to Jenny Youngman, who handled my stories with great care, and to Brenda Lockhart for protecting my time and space to share them.

There are some people in this world who are indispensable companions on the journey. I am grateful to Toska Medlock for championing this project and constantly pushing me to new heights. Thank you for supporting my ministry and for always believing I have something important to offer the world.

My journey to wholeness would not have been possible without the incredible people of Genesis and Saint Mark. I want to thank you for working alongside me and for trusting my vision and leadership. Thank you for standing in the gap for me, most especially in the seasons of depression and grief. I will never forget the Saint Mark staff team for getting on the road to Houston and being there for me when I lost my mom. Thank you most of all for being my family. My love for you, and my sincere gratitude and respect for all that you do to grow the body of Christ, will never, ever leave me.

You think life in a fishbowl is easy? It's difficult being in the spotlight. Thank you, Christina, Wesley, and Janelle, for navigating a host of complex relationships, competing demands, unspoken public expectations, and pastoral emergencies on more than a few holidays. Thank you, Janelle and Wesley, for sharing your dad. I am so proud of both of you. Your constant encouragement taught me the true meaning of authenticity.

INTRODUCTION

"Keep company with me and you'll learn to live freely and lightly."
                —Matthew 11:30, *The Message*

It was the most embarrassing moment of my life. Within the first minute, I knew something was off. I had preached a thousand sermons before and some while feeling under the weather. This time, at a funeral no less, something was different, something was off. I woke up not feeling well that morning, but a pastor doesn't get to fall ill when he or she has to minister to a grieving family. As I prepared for the day, I knew I was feeling tired, fatigued, like this was another thing I would just have to power through.

I remember clearly, I was preaching from Psalm 23, talking about valley experiences. The irony, although I didn't realize it at the time, is that I was approaching a valley of my own. I preached that the Lord provides quiet places and is our shepherd, he leads us by quiet streams and restores our souls. Words of comfort came out of my mouth, but my mind was reeling and fighting to stay present. This grieving family was looking to me for support, much like in my life as a spiritual leader week-in and week-out, and all I wanted to do was be a help to people in need.

I stood in the pulpit, looked at the congregation gathered, and I quickly realized I was not going to make it through the sermon. As I hurried my way through it, looking at this grieving family, in mid-sentence I felt light-headed and disoriented, and then, I went down. The next thing I knew, paramedics were putting me into an ambulance.

On my way to the hospital, I felt embarrassed and ashamed, like a failure. I had let down a family and a community that was depending on me. For a long time, whenever I saw that family, the humiliation I felt about that experience would wash over me. What kind of pastor passes out while preaching a funeral? What could be so wrong with me that it would come to such an extreme example of breakdown? When I got to the hospital, the doctors examined me and gave me a diagnosis I had never heard of: I had "extreme fatigue."

Extreme fatigue. From all outward appearances, things were fine. My new church start, Genesis United Methodist Church, was growing at a rapid pace. We were adding staff to accomplish all the work and ministry to be done. Some of the innovative things our ministry was doing were featured on local news channels. Newspapers were writing about us. We were featured on a segment of the nationally syndicated radio show *The Osgood File*. Because of all the outward appearances of success of my new church, you would think that I was living on a mountaintop. I was telling everyone who would listen about the great things that were going on at Genesis.

But the news didn't tell the story of the pressure I had put on myself to keep the ministry going. I didn't realize it, but I had set such a high standard and expectation for myself that there would be no way to maintain that pace of work. I didn't take time off. I preached every Sunday. I was the spiritual CEO. I was the decision-maker. I was leading this ministry, and that meant 24/7 availability. Outwardly it looked like I was on a mountaintop, and I felt like I was on a mountaintop—for a short while. But then there I was, lying in the back of an ambulance with extreme fatigue. Sadly, what should have been a red light I treated as a yellow light, slowing down only to assess the situation but going right back to work at the same pace that would not be sustainable for me or for any one person.

Mountains and Valleys

The LORD is my shepherd, I lack nothing.
    He makes me lie down in green pastures,
he leads me beside quiet waters,
    he refreshes my soul.
He guides me along the right paths
    for his name's sake.
Even though I walk
    through the darkest valley,
I will fear no evil,
    for you are with me;
your rod and your staff,
    they comfort me.
You prepare a table before me
    in the presence of my enemies.

You anoint my head with oil;
  my cup overflows.
Surely your goodness and love will follow me
  all the days of my life,
and I will dwell in the house of the LORD
  forever. (Ps. 23)

Psalm 23 became a metaphor for the type of shift I would need to make in my own life. I was on a mountaintop, but I was quickly headed toward the valley. At the beginning of Psalm 23 David describes God, telling us who God is. *The Lord* is my shepherd. *He* makes me lie down in green pastures. *He* leads me beside quiet waters. *He* refreshes me. *He* guides me. David is talking *about* God. But when he gets to his valley, David changes from talking about God and starts talking *to* God. *You* are with me. *Your* rod and staff comfort me. *You* prepare a table for me. *You* anoint my head. *Your* goodness and love will follow me. On the mountaintop, it's *easier* to talk about God, isn't it? We shout out that the Lord is good. The Lord has done this for me! But when we find ourselves in the valley, we come face-to-face with God, and our language shifts. We need an intimacy with God deeper than we've known before. We need to rehearse to ourselves and say out loud to God, "You are with me, God. You comfort me, God. You defend me, God. You bless me, God." This is how we take each step through the valley. I had to stop talking *about* God and start talking *right to* God.

You might wonder why I would want you to know about my story. Why would I want to share my journey when it means admitting that I don't have it all together? The reason is because

I believe with all my heart that vulnerability and authenticity are the only way to find wholeness in Jesus Christ. We're not meant to gloss over or skim the surface, pretending our way through life. Jesus invites us to be real with him and with one another. Within the following pages are stories of my depression, despair, burnout, and shame. I'm not here to tell you that followers of Jesus will always have big houses, pain-free living, and all the happiness in the world. It's just not true. I'm not here to tell you that leaders, regardless of the scope of their public platforms, have it all together and never suffer pain, loss, or sadness. I am here to tell you that I believe in the holistic, healing love and salvation in Jesus Christ, who walks with us in the valleys and brings beauty from ash heaps again and again and again. I am here to tell you that I have been on the mountaintops and in the valleys, and I have discovered that we need a reset in our souls. We need to share stories so that others will too. When we're free to be real, that's when the real joy comes.

I have to tell this story because there are so many people who are suffering in silence. It's not just people who lead churches. I've sat in secular leadership training groups with business leaders, heads of universities, civic leaders, and executives of non-profit organizations. I've sat on boards of directors with many public leaders who in private moments can't wait to share with me the pain they are feeling in their own lives. Many of these persons are members of some church. We haven't done a good enough job in the church of being a safe place for vulnerability and authenticity. We put on our church clothes and paint on our smiles, pretending that we're all okay as we praise and worship, only to drive away with the same heavy burdens and struggles we walked in with.

I believe that until we create churches that allow for more authenticity and transparency—where it's okay to not be okay—and people can honestly tell their stories, we'll continue to hear about burnout, stress, depression, anxiety, suicides, exhaustion, and breakdowns. I'm sharing my story because I want to chip away at the stigma around mental health in the church and faith communities. I want you to know my story, to know where I've been and where I'm at now so that we can begin a journey of healing together. I believe that healthy congregations create healthy people and healthy people create healthy congregations. I believe that the core of discipleship is wholeness. I believe in a God of holistic salvation, that God is concerned with saving every aspect of our being—our bodies, our souls, and our minds. I hope my story inspires you to recognize where you are right now, where you want to be, and how to avoid the pitfalls of trying to be everything to everybody. I've discovered that people need a place to be vulnerable and authentic, to know that they are not alone, whatever they may be going through, and that all of us play a role in helping to make churches that kind of safe space.

This runs counter to what we expect and experience in most churches. We think success looks like lots of people showing up, prominence, an environment free of conflict and baggage, tons of programs and activities, where everyone is happy all the time. That was true for Genesis UMC. We were a celebratory place, full of joy and exuberance—new and fresh. I remember a Genesis church member who approached me once to tell me that she was leaving our ministry because our worship experience was too joy-ful. She didn't feel like there was a place for her to express her sadness, so she had to leave. We need places where we can name where we are. We need to create spaces for people to say out loud they are feeling sadness or fatigue, brokenness, or whatever valley they are walking through.

The Bible gives us a roadmap to wholeness. It starts and ends with Jesus, just as this book will. I've discovered that there are many examples of persons in scripture who have found their way through depression, anxiety, and burnout—who have walked through a valley—and found themselves in the embrace of God's relentless love for them and who have lived into God's vision for their lives. We'll look at the experiences of David and what he has to teach us about depression. We'll look at the actions of Mary and Martha to see what they can teach us about stress and feeling overwhelmed. We'll look to Elijah for an examination of exhaus-tion and burnout. We'll study Job's life to learn about grief. We'll explore Judas's and Peter's responses to Jesus' arrest to see what they might teach us about shame, fear, and vulnerability.

This book is a call to reset and regroup. It's an opportunity to name that we're exhausted, overcommitted, chronically fatigued, and depressed; we're working too much; we're ashamed; we're afraid; we feel alone; and we need Jesus. Jesus shows us how to live and how to live life abundantly. I must confess that as a leader, there have been times in my ministry when I've drifted and gone off course. I've carried burdens that didn't belong to me; they belonged to God. I've carried people's problems that didn't belong to me; they belonged to God. I've carried unrealistic views of how others thought a leader should behave, think, and act that didn't belong to me; they belonged to God. I've carried hurt that I should have given to God. I've carried the weight of unrealistic expectations when I should have given them to God. I was operating in my own strength instead of accessing the kingdom resources that are available to me.

Jesus says in Matthew 11:28-30, "Walk with me and work with me—watch how I do it. Learn the unforced rhythms of grace. I won't lay anything heavy or ill-fitting on you. Keep company with me and you'll learn to live freely and lightly" (*The Message*).

My prayer for you is that you will slow down long enough to discover Jesus' unforced rhythms of grace. Jesus offers us a way to live, to lead, and to love that does not end in burnout. I'm convinced that wherever you are on your journey, this book will empower you to allow the work of God's transformation to become a reality in your life.

1

"How Is It with Your Soul?"

"Are you tired? Worn out? Burned out on religion? Come to me. Get away with me and you'll recover your life. I'll show you how to take a real rest. Walk with me and work with me—watch how I do it. Learn the unforced rhythms of grace. I won't lay anything heavy or ill-fitting on you. Keep company with me and you'll learn to live freely and lightly."

—Matthew 11:28-30, *The Message*

Have you ever walked into church checking your watch and saying to yourself, *I'll be out of here in 90 minutes*? Have you walked into a church committee meeting and watched the clock the whole time? If you have, you might be "burned out on religion"!

If we're honest, most of us have had seasons like that. In order to reset our souls and experience the wholeness we crave, we need only look to Jesus. He showed us how to be in ministry, how

23

to work long hours, how to address the needs and expectations of many people, all while staying connected to God. He knows that it's all too easy to get burned out on religion. He knows that taking a real rest is rarely easy to do. He knows that we need to recover our lives. He knows how we feel and what we go through because he has lived it. God came to us in Jesus Christ and walked our steps, felt our feelings, experienced everything that we go through. He is the path to wholeness.

What Is Wholeness?

As you begin to think about your own soul reset, I invite you to use the words of Matthew 11:28-30 as a definition of *wholeness*. The invitation from Jesus is to stay close to him and learn to live freely and lightly. Close your eyes for a few seconds and just imagine a feeling of living free and light. What does that mean for you? When was the last time you felt free or light? When was the last time you felt really close to Jesus? When was the last time you felt whole—in your body, mind, and spirit?

In my experience, discovering wholeness has required practicing the means of grace. Means of grace are those intentional practices that put us squarely in the flow of grace—practices such as prayer, silence, solitude, confession, journaling, physical exercise, small groups, worship, and practicing the presence of God, to name a few. I've had to intentionally create habits and rhythms that keep me close to Jesus in order to maintain any lasting sense of wholeness. I've also had to unlearn the idea that going to church on Sundays counted as my only time with God for the week. Going to corporate worship is one means of grace and is an important practice. But if we're not seeking God daily, we will not experience the fullness of life Jesus offers to us. Practicing the means of grace isn't always something we do inside the church; it's also something we do in our daily lives and in our relationships. We have to choose to spend time with God every single day, pursuing healing and wholeness that leads to light and free living.

When we do experience wholeness, we find capacity to handle difficult life situations and stress because we are connected to Jesus. It doesn't mean we are free from trials, but it does mean that we have the capacity to handle them. It means that God's love, mercy, and kindness sustain us through whatever we face. When we are growing in Christ and Christ is in us, we discover a joy that isn't manufactured or dependent upon external circumstances. That joy is at our core and isn't easily shaken.

Wholeness looks like the ability to be able to share Christ out of our abundance because we are so close to Jesus that his grace and love have filled us up to the point that it overflows from us to others. Pursuing wholeness has led me to freedom from a façade. I'm not pretending to have it all together anymore. Seeking wholeness has trained me to live in very authentic, organic, consistent ways. I live with integrity and can be my true self; I'm not hiding from anybody. I've discovered that God's love for me is not dependent upon my productivity or my positivity. Because I am close to Jesus, I can be vulnerable, and my vulnerability might help others on their spiritual journey. There is no substitute for closeness with Jesus on this soul reset journey. He is the first thing, the last thing, and everything in between!

The First Thing

My son graduated from the University of Kansas with a degree in sports journalism. He loves baseball, but I have no idea where he got his love of the game. I hate baseball. Games are long and slow and boring. When I ask him why he likes baseball so much, he goes on and on about how baseball games have so much happening at once. There's strategy and analytics and nuance about every last detail—who's hitting, who's pitching, who's on base, who's playing shortstop; it's all working together for good (or bad) in any given game. I'm thinking, *That's all going on while I'm staring at the TV just waiting—no,* begging—*for something to happen.* I'm bored to tears watching, but my son watches with excitement, and he says to me, "You know, Dad, when these guys get up to bat and one of them gets a hit, it's exciting! Everyone's watching to see how far he can run or whether he'll beat the throw to first." Then my son said something that stuck with me: He reminded me that the most important thing for that hitter as he takes off for first base is that he must *touch the bag* at first base. "If he misses the bag, nothing else matters. If he rounds all the bases but forgets to the touch the first-base bag, he's out. Nothing counts." If you don't touch first base, nothing matters. If you hit the ball into the outfield and miss first base, it's not a hit. If you make it all the way home, but you don't touch first base, you don't get the home run.

My pastor senses picked up on this, and it occurred to me that the same is true for the Christian life. If we do all the things we're supposed to do—if we serve the church well, share our faith, and do all the things we're supposed to do for Jesus—but we don't do the first thing, then we actually haven't gotten anywhere at all. The most important thing—our first-base tag—is staying close to Jesus. Waking up with him. Walking through our days with him. Serving with him. Loving our family and friends with him. Eating with him. Resting in him. The first thing is our closeness to Jesus. That's what sustains us for the lives and the works to which we are called.

I don't know about you, but I needed to get back to the first thing, my first love, Jesus. I literally had a breakdown before I remembered that Jesus offers an abundant life and unforced rhythms of grace. It took a crisis for me to realize that I hadn't tapped the bag at first base. Instead, I was building my life and ministry on what I could produce *for* Jesus. I was leading a thriving, growing, dynamic church and celebrating all kinds of statistical successes—all the while working myself into depression, anxiety, and breakdown. In my work as the General Secretary/CEO for Discipleship Ministries of The United Methodist Church, I've found that's where a lot of believers live—depressed, anxious, and on the verge of a breakdown. Many of us, if not most, in the church have forgotten why we do what we do in the first place. We've forgotten that the message of Jesus is actually good news of freedom, hope, and possibility, not just more things to accomplish, programs to run, and busyness to get swept up in. Especially for pastors and church leaders, we get focused on numbers, budgets, growth, and programs because those are the "measurables." But we forget that Jesus invited us into a life-changing relationship, a companionship meant to bring wholeness. Our forgetfulness creates anxiety and busyness, and we get stuck in that space of anxiety instead of living the abundant life.

I want to be very clear that I'm speaking from experience. I'm not just preaching to you a sermon about life change or spiritual awakening. I'm giving you my testimony. You see, I lost sight of my "why." What turned out to be a very simple proposition—to plant a church that would reach new people—turned into external and institutional pressures. When I was beginning the work of planting a church, no one ever asked me, "Hey, Junius, how is it with your soul?" The questions I got asked time and again were, "How many people are coming?" "What's your budget up to?" "When are you going to buy land and build a building?" I didn't have a chance to think about my personal time with Jesus; I had to stay focused on getting this church off the ground in order to have good answers to those questions. Somewhere along the way, my starting point shifted from growing in relationship with God and helping other people grow in their relationships with God and instead turned to institutional tasks like numbers, money, growth, and so on. I had lost sight of the *why* without even realizing it, and I began to feel more and more isolated and disconnected. Numbers and budgets and property are all important aspects of a church plant, to be sure, but not at the expense of the *why*—that closeness to Jesus Christ. As my priorities became a matter of just trying to keep the thing afloat, I drifted off course in my spiritual life. I became more and more spiritually scattered, and less and less spiritually whole.

Of course, it is possible both to attend to the numbers and to live an abundant life. But it only works with a reservoir of Living

Water, staying deeply rooted in the *why*. That's when numbers and budgets generate joy, purpose, and hunger for the things we get to do as a part of the body of Christ. Absent that, we are just engaging in church tasks and chores without passion and without energy for the road ahead—and let me tell you, that does not turn out well. Jesus has called us to learn from him, to be his apprentices in order to be his disciples. We learn from him how to live as he did so that we can be his disciples in the world today.

Reclaiming Discipleship

When we get back to our first thing, we see that everything comes back to discipleship. Jesus called his disciples to follow him and to learn from him; and before he ascended to heaven, he called us all to discipleship when he told us to take the gospel to the whole world. When we begin to really understand what a disciple is—a person who knows Christ, who is growing in Christ, who is serving Christ and sharing Christ—we discover that discipleship is a lifelong journey that requires a steady connectedness to Jesus.

How often have you considered your call as a disciple of Jesus Christ? How often have you made intentional choices to grow as a disciple of Jesus? I had life plans for career, for retirement, and for finances—but I never had a spiritual growth plan. What about you? Do you have a spiritual growth plan? I came to realize that I focus on that which I give attention to. We tend to feed our focus. I'll be the first to admit that there have been many seasons in my leadership when I did not prioritize my own spiritual life, even as I was encouraging the people in my churches to do the same. I've discovered that leadership is first and foremost leadership of oneself. As a leader, discipleship begins with me. My soul's connectedness to Jesus is first base. If I don't make a plan to take care of myself, there is no way I'll be any good to anyone, nor will I be able to lead anyone else to Jesus.

Sadly, I believe that we have twisted and turned around the whole idea of what discipleship is in the church. We've created more programs and things to sign up for, calling them discipleship, instead of inviting people to wholeness in Jesus and growing in abundant life, all day and every day. Growing as a disciple isn't about finding more things to do at church; it's about my very being becoming like Christ, representing Christ. I believe we need fewer church activities and more people living light and free abundant lives.

"How Is It with Your Soul?"

John Wesley, the founder of Methodism, taught us a question that we use as a tool to continually check our priorities, our sense of wholeness, and bring us back to our first thing. He would have us ask ourselves and one another, "How is it with your soul?" Friends, our churches have to be places where this is a safe question to answer. We have to tell the truth about where we are spiritually so that we can encourage one another and point one another back to Jesus.

I've heard that the number-one cause of stress is incongruent values—not being authentic, not living out what you think is truly important. If you think following Jesus is important but your life doesn't have any room for time with him, things might start to feel forced and burdensome. That's stressful!

This is what I believe Jesus was talking about when he described living in abundance. When he said, "Seek ye first the kingdom of God," he was telling us to touch first base! Seek God first, he said, and all the other things will be added. We want to jump to home base without seeking first, don't we? We want influence and popularity, persuasion, positioning, wealth, and so on. But we've got to seek God first in order to really live the unforced rhythms of the spiritual life.

Remembering the *Why*

If you're reading this book, I'm going to make an assumption that you want to grow as a disciple of Jesus Christ. Maybe you're someone who is responsible for helping to lead others to grow. Maybe you're gathered with a small group of friends who are seeking to grow in discipleship and in community. I want to ask you to think about your call to follow Jesus, when you first accepted Christ. Think about the feelings you experienced, the zeal you had for Jesus, and the closeness you felt to him. I confess that I can get too busy doing the work of the church and forget the Great Commission: *Go and make disciples.* We've got to ask ourselves and each other: "How are you doing that?" And the reason can't be "because I want a larger congregation" or more power or influence. Our why is that we are called to make disciples.

I remember being in a consultation with a group of church leaders, talking about next steps in their ministries. As we were talking about those next steps, I lifted up the vision of helping people grow in their relationship with Jesus Christ. One of the leaders shared very candidly, "I started with that desire, but I'm so far from that. The only thing I'm concerned about at this point is how do I get more volunteers. How do I keep this ministry going?" Her honest reflection was not a complaint but a lament. She had lost her why and had gotten swept up in the business of ministry. The expectations of her leadership created a seductive shift from "being" to "doing." I invited her and the rest of the group to spend some time reconnecting with the why of their leadership. When you have clarity about your why, it brings what you are doing into sharper focus. It reignites your passion for Jesus and for ministry. Do you know *your* why?

I discovered my personal why when I came of age as a teenager at Windsor Village UMC in Houston, Texas. That was the first time the Word of God became flesh in my life. I became deeply connected to God and felt clearly the call God had placed on my life. That experience got me connected not just to the church but to the living God and gave me a framework for how I'd live my life and lead others. It gave me a framework for the power of Christian community. That same why led me to go plant a new church.

This is why I teach churches the phrase "Discipleship begins with me." You cannot teach what you do not know. You cannot model what you do not practice. You cannot lead where you're not willing to go. This is such an important concept for being a well-grounded, spiritually whole, and healthy leader.

Leadership is first and foremost leadership of oneself. Lead yourself well, because how you lead yourself shapes how you lead others. How you lead yourself shapes how you relate to others and engage the world. Because this is such a cyclical thing and a relational journey we are on, people lead as they have experienced being led.

I have shared many times with leaders who are preparing for an important meeting, "You may have a tough meeting tonight. People have been working all day, and there may be some disgruntled people who are anxious or fearful of whatever we're dealing with. Go spend some time taking care of yourself. Go to a movie or to the gym. Listen to a song that inspires you. Get into a healthy headspace. Someone in the room needs to be centered."

When I become irritable and short with people, I know these are warning signs that I need time alone with God. When I get frustrated easily, then I know I'm running off course. I know that when I see red flags, the answer is not *let me plan this other thing or read another book.* My plan is, go be with God. Reconnect with God and reset. Then, I have the capacity to handle what's in front of me. The answer will always be going back to the center—to God. That will increase your capacity to do what you need to do.

In the next chapter, I'll share more with you about just how desperately I have needed wholeness in Jesus Christ. I learned that freedom and authenticity go together. When we tell the truth about the burdens we bear, it's easier to lay them down and learn how to live freely and lightly. We just have to watch how Jesus does it.

Soul Reset Practice

Take a few minutes to spend in the spiritual practice of journaling. If you don't have a journal, grab a notepad, or start a note on your computer or phone. Let your heart guide your fingers as you write or type. Listen to God and write your thoughts without fear of judgment or criticism. Just talk to God. Consider where you are spiritually, right now in this very moment. Are you feeling overburdened? Are you feeling deep joy? Are you on a mountaintop or in a valley? What do you need to say to God? What do you need to hear from God? Read Matthew 11:28-30 and reflect on how your heart and soul respond to these words from Jesus. What do you need to let go of in order to live lightly and freely?

Reflection Questions

1. *Reflect on the story about the importance of touching the bag at first base. How does the idea of needing to get back to your first thing resonate in your soul?*
2. *How do you define wholeness? When have you felt a sense of wholeness? When have you felt less than whole?*
3. *How is it with your soul right now? What do you need from God? What do you need from your community?*

⏻ The daily spiritual practice for this week is **Examen**. Turn to page 109 to discover ways to practice *examen* every day in the coming week.

2

When Depression Hit

My tears have been my food
  day and night,
while people say to me all day long,
  "Where is your God?"

—Psalm 42:3

W hat do you have to be depressed about?" These soul-piercing words came from a colleague after I had shared what was really going on with me emotionally, physically, and spiritually. In a rare moment of vulnerability, when I was asked, "How are you?", I took a risk. I told the truth. I said, "I'm not feeling good at all. I'm worried about some things. I'm afraid things are going to fall apart. I'm feeling extremely down."

What do you have to be depressed about? Honestly, I had asked myself the same question many times. What *did* I have to be depressed about? By all outward appearances, things were going fine with me. My new church start was going great. I had given every drop of sweat and every ounce of energy—everything I had—to make it the best it could be. We were growing and thriving, by all measures a smashing success. But my body and soul were showing signs of road wear. I remember several times driving throughout my day when I would come to a stoplight and just start crying, wondering what in the world was wrong with me. I didn't know how quickly I was burning out until one Thursday morning that I will never forget.

The Sunday before this particular Thursday, I had preached, greeted people before and after church, written down some details from conversations I didn't want to lose track of during the upcoming week, and had my family time—seemingly a successful Sunday. But by Monday morning, I found myself unable to get out of bed; like, literally, I could not move from the bed. Although Monday morning was my normal day to rest, I knew I was feeling something different, something out of the ordinary. I felt the same way on Tuesday. I called my office to say that I wouldn't be in. I didn't eat or sleep. I just lay in bed, crying in darkness, with my blinds shut. So Tuesday came and went; same thing. Then Wednesday came and went. By Thursday, I called my wife at work and asked her to come home. I told her that I was still in bed, again, and that I needed her home. She came home and asked me, "What's wrong? What's happening to you?" I sobbed uncontrollably. I didn't know what was happening to me; I just knew that I had hit a wall. I knew I needed immediate intervention. That same day, we found a psychologist, and I told her I was in crisis and needed an appointment. She heard my sense of urgency and opened a spot for me immediately.

When I met my new (and first-ever) therapist, I was pleased to discover that she happened to be the spouse of a pastor. As I introduced myself to her and began to tell my story, she immediately identified with my experience and my context. She knew what it meant to live life in a public spotlight. She knew what my life was like with all its demands. I shared that my normal rhythm of life and work was completely turned upside down, that I could no longer function. I literally could not keep going at the pace and productivity level I had been. My body physically could not go on anymore. My emotions were spiraling out of control. My spiritual life was drying up. My therapist, in her wisdom, diagnosed an emotional breakdown. *An emotional breakdown.* I was clinically depressed. The diagnosis resonated right away, but as I left her office that day, I did have to wonder, *How did I get here?*

Starting out in my ministry, I remember sitting in a new church start training and hearing a pastor share about how he had gotten to a place of burnout and depression. I couldn't imagine how anyone could ever experience depression amid all the exciting aspects of a new ministry. I remember saying to myself, naively, *That will never happen to me.* However, we don't know what we don't know. After my breakdown, I began to understand more about depression. I came to realize that there are some different types of depression: episodic, where something triggers a depressive episode; and a chemical imbalance, with which every day is a fight for joy. Learning about depression with my therapist became an *aha!* moment for me: I discovered that this wasn't the first time I had experienced depression in my life, but it was the first time I had recognized it and called it by name.

I first experienced depression as a teenager in junior high school. I was part of a group of students who were bused to a predominantly white school in Houston, Texas. It was called a "minority to majority transfer." I was excited about the opportunity for a new academic experience and going to a new school. But not all of my new classmates and teachers were very happy about our presence on campus. It was a hostile environment, to say the least. That was the first time I remember experiencing overt racism, and it affected me in a very profound way.

The first semester of my eighth-grade year was a complete blur. I spent every day after school in my room sleeping. I didn't want to eat, go outside and play, watch TV, or engage with others. I just wanted to sleep. I nearly failed every class. My mother knew something was wrong beyond the normal lack of motivation in a lot of teenagers. At this point, she became an advocate for my academic and emotional well-being. She demanded that I be taken out of that school, and I was re-enrolled in the school to which I originally had been zoned. Slowly my emotional state improved, and I began to flourish in a new environment.

Now that I know what depression is, it's easy to look back and see that depression has been with me for a very long time.

A Turning Point

As I explored my condition with my new therapist, I realized that my emotional breakdown meant that I needed a reset. I would need regular counseling sessions, a renovation of my work routine, a full examination of the state of my soul . . . and medication. I'll never forget the language my counselor used as she prescribed to me a medication she said would "take the weights off my shoulders," so that I could do the internal work I needed to do. It wasn't going to be immediate, and there was no quick fix. This wasn't a cure or a magic pill, but it would give me the space to work on *me* and lift the weight long enough for me to do the work I needed to do in order to be healthy and whole. I had never seen a therapist before, but this image of carrying a heavy weight resonated deeply with me. I had read the scriptures where Jesus says his burden is light, but the burden I carried around was anything but light. My counselor and I began to talk about creating some kind of balance in my work life. I didn't know what that meant. My whole life was ministry, and that was all I knew. It was time for me to examine how I was living my life.

Now, I want to be sure to say a word about medication. We need to do some work on peeling back the stigma of medications for emotional and mental health. Sometimes in order to climb out of the darkness, we need help—we need the weight off of our shoulders so we can begin the climb. I needed help, something beyond just "Pray harder" or "Pray longer." In the church, we sometimes tend to super-spiritualize things to a point where we create a taboo around mental illness. This prevents many of us from publicly sharing where we are because of the stigma associated with depression and antidepressants. Don't get me wrong, I firmly believe in the power of prayer. I believe that when a person has an illness, we absolutely pray, but there are times when illness requires medicine. I believe that God heals through doctors and medicine and surgeries, but that healing comes from God.

We get confused when we think we can't take a prescription because it would mean we don't trust God enough. I believe in a holistic salvation. What I mean by this is that God heals through various means. God doesn't just save us for heaven in the future. God saves our hearts and souls and bodies in the here and now. God cares about our whole person, just as we are. I find it so liberating to praise God for a pill that will lift the weight off my shoulders so that God can do the work God needs to do in my soul.

As I began to journey through my depression, I was forced to do things differently. I had to have difficult conversations with my church leaders, sharing with them where I was emotionally and spiritually. I had to admit that I was struggling. I had to be vulnerable and say, "I've hit a wall that is affecting my ability to lead effectively." When they might have been disappointed in me or discouraged by their leader's weaknesses, instead, my church leaders said, "Don't worry about it, we got you." That was one of the first moments of vulnerability in my ministry when I had to admit where I was emotionally and spiritually. I had to publicly admit that I was human, and I will never forget the grace that met me in that space.

My tears have been my food
    day and night,
while people say to me all day long,
    "Where is your God?"

These things I remember
    as I pour out my soul:
how I used to go to the house of God
    under the protection of the Mighty One
with shouts of joy and praise
    among the festive throng.

Why, my soul, are you downcast?
    Why so disturbed within me?
Put your hope in God,
    for I will yet praise him,
    my Savior and my God.

My soul is downcast within me;
    therefore I will remember you
from the land of the Jordan,
    the heights of Hermon—from Mount Mizar.
Deep calls to deep
    in the roar of your waterfalls;
all your waves and breakers
    have swept over me.

By day the LORD directs his love,
    at night his song is with me—
    a prayer to the God of my life.

I say to God my Rock,
    "Why have you forgotten me?
Why must I go about mourning,
    oppressed by the enemy?"

My bones suffer mortal agony
    as my foes taunt me,
saying to me all day long,
    "Where is your God?"

Why, my soul, are you downcast?
    Why so disturbed within me?
Put your hope in God,
    for I will yet praise him,
    my Savior and my God.
                (Ps. 42:3-11)

Where Is God?

In the depth of my depression, I encountered Psalm 42 and found a kindred spirit in David, whom I came to discover also had a season of depression. Psalm 42 resonates so deeply with me because I really do believe that David experienced depression. Those days I lay in bed day after day, wondering what in the world was wrong with me, I could have written David's reflection, "My tears have been my food day and night." Both enemies and friends alike taunted, "Where is your God?" "Why are you depressed?" I've been asked those questions and have even asked them of myself.

I see myself in David: He's writing out of a deep-seated depression. David doesn't know how to handle what he's going through. He is basically a mess and is fixated on what has gone wrong; people taunt him, he is desperate and depressed. I see him looking horizontally at everything falling apart around him instead of looking vertically to God for strength, sustaining grace, and a new beginning. How many times do we get stuck looking at people getting under our skin or at all that is wrong instead of looking to God for strength?

David gets to his most desperate place when there are no more tears to cry, and that's when he remembers. He remembers how he used to go with joy into the house of God. He remembers what it feels like to have walked closely with God, dancing for joy at the greatness of God. He remembers how worship drives him back to the goodness of God time and again. He remembers worship, true worship, full of joy and celebration because he has known God's rescue and restoration.

David's soul was longing for God, and our souls long for God too. No matter what's happening around us, at our core, our souls long for God. We were created with a longing for relationship with the Creator. We long to feel God moving in our lives. We long to experience the joy and peace that come only from God, from a relationship with Jesus. We long to feel the presence of God, where we know that we are being saturated by the love of God.

What David describes in Psalm 42 is what I call "spiritual dehydration." His soul is dehydrated. That's what happens to us when we neglect the core spiritual practices in our lives: We get dehydrated because we lose access to our water source—the Living Water. We can get to a place where we are just going through the motions of a life with God, where worship is just a thing, an event, a once-a-week fix. But sticking our toes into the stream won't satisfy a deep thirst. We have to drink deeply from the well of life.

Part of breaking the chains of depression is reconnecting to God—to the source of Living Water. We remember what we know to be true about the God who loves us so much:

> My tears have been my food
> 　day and night,
> while people say to me all day long,
> 　"Where is your God?" (Ps. 42:3)

Those voices of doubt and discord get more power in our lives when we are not connected to God. They begin to have more power and more influence, and we begin to give those things more credence than we should because we aren't connected to God. Circumstances speak louder and conflict has more power when we're not connected to God. When we are dealing with family issues, financial issues, health issues, those voices begin to creep in, and before we know it, they can lead us into depression. We've got to remember that worship isn't something that we do once a week but a lifestyle. Worshiping God is not about a place but a person. It's not about geography; it's about intimacy.

These things I remember . . . David remembers, he recalls his first love; and we can remember—call to mind what we know of God. That's what I had to do in my depression. I remembered the moments of worshiping God. I remembered what it felt like to be in the presence of God. I remembered the peace that passes all understanding. I remembered those moments of thanksgiving. I remembered. And as David remembers, then he's able to ask himself, *Why am I depressed?* He starts encouraging himself. *I serve a God who delivers, who heals, who brings peace, who brings clarity, who brings understanding, who brings wholeness.* David begins to encourage himself by remembering.

That's what I did too. I had to remember my center. I had to remember that my call was to love God and to love others. I also had to remember the call to love myself. That was the thing that got me back, that helped me to reset my life. I had to go back to the basics—for me, not for other people—by remembering that nobody in my life needs God more than I do.

Yet Praise

My favorite thing about this psalm of David, Psalm 42, is his "yet praise." He shifts from despair to praise, as if to say, "Even here in the pit of depression and desolation, yet will I praise the God who is good and faithful, no matter what I'm facing." I have learned to have a "yet praise" mentality when I feel depression setting in. No matter what I'm experiencing in my life, I say, "Yet will I praise him." How do you get to a "yet praise" point in your life? You get there by remembering—by encouraging yourself, by talking yourself past pain and pressure, by remembering that God has been faithful and good, and that God will be again. You operate in expectancy with a new sense of hope. And even as I was crying day and night, I had a "yet praise" mindset because of what I expected God to do in my life. With whatever strength I had in me, I was going to praise God.

Friends, the strongest voice in your life has to be the voice of God. When other voices have more power, that's the road to being a people-pleaser, to becoming depressed and overwhelmed, to carrying your own heavy burdens. David gets to his "yet praise" and fights back depression. He fights back with worship. He fights back with praise. He fights back by getting back to the center. As he remembers who God is and who he, David, is, he rises with a new perspective.

For me, a new perspective began with my own path to spiritual wholeness. It began with how I saw myself and the importance of my spiritual journey. That would lead to a new perspective on ministry, but I didn't start with the ministry. I started with me and with my own spiritual health. I declared that I may not be able to praise God with *what is* right now, but I will praise God for *what is to come*—the "yet praise."

Being in God's presence is the emotional lifter, but being in God's presence doesn't just happen at church. When you are feeling overwhelmed by financial pressure, it's time to worship. When you are feeling like a failure after a broken relationship, it's time to worship. When life is crushing in on you, it's time to worship. When you're surrounded by a set of circumstances that threatens your faith, it's time to worship. Worship is a lifestyle that reminds us of our ability to "yet praise" in the midst of difficulties.

Time to Reset

At the point of my depression, my life was so out of balance that I neglected spiritual practices. I didn't have a regular routine of meeting with God, just simply to be in God's presence. Of course, I was in the Word regularly to prepare for my sermons or to teach, but rarely was I reading scripture just to hear from God—to get a word just for me. If I was going to experience a new season in my life, a season of refreshing and walking by the quiet, still waters, then I had to do things differently. I was going to have to attend to my own walk with God.

I would have to discover a new sense of balance by making a plan for personal spiritual growth and development. I needed to be in the Word not just to get content for sermons but to spend time in God's word for *me*, not for anybody else. I needed to worship not merely to do the planning of worship; I needed to listen to other pastors' and churches' worship experiences so I could be centered and begin to lead from a place of overflow instead of drought. I discovered that I needed to exercise and eat properly, that caring for my body had much to do with my mental and spiritual health. And most of all, I discovered that the way I lead directly influences the health of the people I lead. People lead as they experience being led. So, I'm now on a journey to lead my team well, to be the first one to admit my struggles, to preach a journey of spiritual practice, and to point to a God who redeems and restores.

It's hard to be vulnerable without fear of judgment. People project what success looks like onto each of us, and it keeps us isolated from one another. We don't share with one another what's really going on in our lives because we're afraid of being judged or misunderstood. We start believing that criticism equals failure and worthlessness. We don't let leaders admit any areas of weakness in their lives. Leaders get confused and think that they have to be loved and accepted by everyone to experience fulfillment. We forget that no matter how successful people are or how effective they are in leadership, we are all human beings who experience brokenness and moments of doubt, moments of discouragement. We're human beings who need words of affirmation and appreciation.

Soul Reset Practice

I want to invite you to take an assessment of your spiritual life at this present moment. Are you connected to the source of Living Water? Are you living and leading from a place of overflow or drought? Is your soul feeling dehydrated? Have tears been your food both day and night? Are you wondering where your God is? I want you to know that I have been to that desert and stumbled through it. I am on the other side and have discovered that the key to deep and abiding joy no matter what is happening to you or around you—the key is drinking deeply from the well of Living Water. The key is connectedness to God who sustains, heals, redeems, and restores. The key is a regular rhythm of spiritual practice—intentional, focused time with God to ask questions, to listen, to love God, and to be loved by God. The key is listening to your body as it tells you what it needs from you regarding nutrition and fitness. The key is listening to the Spirit, who tells you to slow down and to set down your heavy burdens.

A life with God is not meant to be a burden. In fact, it's the opposite. Jesus invites us into a life with God that is light with an easy burden. If you're feeling heavy or burdened, set down that weight and reset your spiritual rhythm. Spend some time in prayer, laying down your burdens and listening to God tell you that you are loved deeply. Step into grace, mercy, and a new start, staying close to the One who will show you the way.

Reflection Questions

1. *Read Psalm 42. Where do you see examples of David in a period of depression? What does David's lament teach us about sadness, depression, and honesty with God?*
2. *Do you agree that there is a stigma around mental illness and medications for mental illnesses? Why or why not? If you do agree, what can we do to get rid of that stigma?*
3. *When have you needed to "yet praise" God in the middle of difficult seasons of your life?*
4. *How does worship lift up our hearts?*
5. *What are some spiritual practices that can nurture our souls, bodies, and minds? Which of these speak most directly to you, and why?*

The daily spiritual practice for this week is ***Prayer***. Turn to page 112 to discover ways to practice prayer every day in the coming week.

3

It's Not All on Me

"Martha, Martha," the Lord answered, "you are worried and upset about many things, but few things are needed—or indeed only one. Mary has chosen what is better, and it will not be taken away from her."

—Luke 10:41-42

When I had a dream to plant a church, I imagined forming creative and innovative ways for reaching people to connect with Jesus. That was my goal, pointing people to Jesus. But my denomination needed a new church, which meant that there would be systems and structures to set up, plans and goals I'd have to make, and benchmarks to meet. There was monetary investment from the denomination, so I needed to produce results to keep it going. I'd quickly learn that balancing the institutional demands and the pure desire of wanting people to meet Jesus would prove a tricky task. The more I walked the line between those two goals, the more stressed and overwhelmed I became.

I deeply wanted to be with Jesus and point people to him, but I also had to produce a result; there were so many tasks to get done.

Reflecting on those early days, I realize that it never occurred to me that I could fail. Early on, I wasn't stressed or overwhelmed. I wasn't afraid of failure, and I never even considered our little ministry effort not making it off the ground. Once I started really connecting with people, groups started forming, and my team came into place. We had a launch date and a place to worship. We had some struggles, but we weren't stressed yet. My stress came when we started succeeding. Then it became, *Wow! How am I going to keep this thing going?*

I know many leaders who wrestle with this type of stress. I was having dinner with someone who has been very successful in leading change in organizations. I'll call her Emily. Emily is an entrepreneur who started and built a multimillion-dollar company in her industry. She is a trusted person I turn to for help and perspective when I'm making major decisions about leadership and change. We were having casual conversation about this book project that drifted to me telling the story of my journey in ministry. I talked about stress and depression. I also talked about the pressure of leadership, especially in the public arena, and all the sleepless nights that accompany trying just to keep things going. She listened intently.

What happened next surprised me. Emily didn't offer me any sage advice. She didn't express shock or judgment about my journey. Instead, she paused and began to share her own story with me. I was amazed at how eerily similar our experiences in leadership were. I was quickly reminded of the emotional toll that leading others can inflict on people regardless of their profession. My conversation with Emily fueled my passion to complete this book. She taught me that so many of us face the reality and the stress of trying to focus on the right things, even in a successful venture.

In my moments of extreme stress and anxiety in the early days of my ministry, my tendency was to go quickly into problem-solving mode. I would usually ask my staff, "What do I need to do more of?" Not only was I raising my level of anxiety and my stress level but also I was raising the level of stress of the people working with me. I stressed everyone out to the point where somebody said to me, "Junius, we're doing the right things. We don't need to do more of anything, we just need to keep doing these right things—community engagement, great worship, deep small groups." Those were the things we were focused on, but I still felt tremendous pressure whenever anyone asked how many people were coming to our services. To this day, I never start a conversation with any pastor related to how many people are coming. I've learned not to ask institutional questions but instead to ask spiritual ones. "How's your soul?" "How are you taking care of yourself?" "What's your *why* behind all of your effort?" "Are you staying connected to Jesus?"

Doing the Right Things

New stresses will always present themselves in whatever venture we find ourselves a part of, but we have to keep asking ourselves: *What are the right things to be doing?* You can always add more to your plate, but if we keep focused on the *right* things, we'll be much healthier in our attempt to reset.

I thought we were focused on the right things at church. But I sure wasn't focused on the right things in my own life. My schedule became a beast. My family time began to shrink. Church became all-consuming. Even though the church was focused on the right things, I wasn't. Instead of paying attention to what was happening to my spirit, I just kept adding and adding. Anytime there was a gap in leadership, I filled in and had way too much on my plate. I became busier and busier to the point of becoming completely overwhelmed. In the early days of my ministry, I never would have thought that three years later I would collapse at a funeral. I guess you'd never anticipate such a dramatic display of exhaustion.

My California church had many new believers attending, and my job was to point them to Jesus. But soon, I began to take on the burden of things that were going on in their lives. I would take it personally if someone had doubts about God or hadn't come to church in a while. I felt responsible for their ongoing journey with God, like I hadn't made a compelling-enough case or as if I hadn't created enough connection points for them to lock in to our community. Of course, now I know that it was never my responsibility to save anyone, only to point them to Christ and to give them opportunities that would help them grow. It wasn't my job to *make* them grow or even to make the church grow. My job was to point to Jesus. But I started to feel like the whole church depended on *me*. I became a rescuer. I didn't let people fail because I didn't want the church to fail. If you're a pastor reading this, maybe you can relate. Or if you're a church member reading this, perhaps you've seen pastors take on the weight of the whole world until they are crushed by it. If you're the owner of a business or an executive in your company, maybe you can relate to the weight of feeling overly responsible for every aspect of the operation.

Here's what I discovered about my need to fix and rescue: I had basically short-circuited the ability to learn from failures. In community we fail together, we learn from it, and we move on together. But I couldn't let the failures happen, so I took on burdens that didn't belong to me. Deep down, I could not allow myself to fully trust the capacity of my leaders—even though they were super-capacity kind of people. But they showed me over and over again that not only could they be trusted—they also should be celebrated for their great leadership.

Since our new church had been alive, I had preached every single Sunday. But in the second summer of our church's life, when we had to find a temporary spot because of renovation at the middle-school gym where we had been worshiping, I finally decided to take a Sunday off. Naturally, an opportunity for great leadership would present itself the day I took a vacation. I called our facilities person to ask how the church service had gone that morning at the temporary location. He told me that the person who was supposed to have let them in at this different place never showed up. Of course, I immediately freaked out, but he cut me off to say, "Everything went great, we just had worship in the parking lot."

If I had been there, I would have robbed everyone of that amazing opportunity. I would have panicked and gotten on the phone and tried to make something happen. But they knew the right thing to do was just to set up for worship, right there in the parking lot. So that left me with a new realization—that I have to consider what belongs to me, what belongs to others, and what belongs to God. I can't carry burdens that don't belong to me. We have to have opportunities to fail in order to grow. I don't need to be the rescuer. My team set up worship in the parking lot! What was I worried about? They did not need me to be a rescuer.

This, of course, is the challenge we face daily as believers. Our faith teaches us to care for others. But caring can be an unlimited concept. It is possible to care to the point that we become more harmful than helpful. We begin to take on the role of "god" in someone's life. I believe when we are fully connected to Jesus as Savior and practicing spiritual disciplines daily, it grows our capacity to discern where our responsibility for others ends and theirs begins. Staying focused on the right things in our personal lives frees us for joyful and abundant living. I have personally witnessed many people who headed down the road to burnout and depression because they didn't have the ability to stay focused on the right things.

Stress and Busyness

My busyness turned to stress, which turned to a feeling of being completely overwhelmed. I didn't even know how stressed out I was, trying to do the things I thought I had to do in order to be a successful pastor and an effective leader. My schedule was so jam-packed that there wasn't a single moment of margin to just be with God. I was attempting to respond to demands that I and others put on me. The result was a life filled with stress and worry. I wonder how many of us operate out of a place of stress and chaos instead of surrender and peace. To be sure, there are things to be done, tasks to accomplish. But how could we, the church, lead the way in living lightly and freely as Jesus followers in the world? How could we, the church, lead people to Jesus by our witness of practicing the presence of God—which is simply keeping company with God all day, every day, in and out of daily routines? Look with me at the story of Jesus' visit to Mary and Martha's house, to consider how we might have clear eyes to see what the next right thing is.

As Jesus and his disciples were on their way, he came to a village where a woman named Martha opened her home to him. She had a sister called Mary, who sat at the Lord's feet listening to what he said. But Martha was distracted by all the preparations that had to be made. She came to him and asked, "Lord, don't you care that my sister has left me to do the work by myself? Tell her to help me!"

"Martha, Martha," the Lord answered, "you are worried and upset about many things, but few things are needed—or indeed only one. Mary has chosen what is better, and it will not be taken away from her." (Luke 10:38-42)

Mary and Martha demonstrated what it means to tend to the right things when they found themselves entertaining Jesus and his disciples in their house. Mary knew the place to be right at that moment was seated next to Jesus, soaking up every bit of time she could get. Her priority was closeness to Jesus. Martha expressed her love for Jesus by *doing*. She couldn't get past all that had to be done before she could relax and just be with Jesus. Martha was busy doing the work of hospitality. Who doesn't want to ensure that everything is just right for their guests? The power of this story is that it continues to be played out in our lives. We are so busy trying to do the work of the gospel that we often fail to slow down long enough to simply soak it in.

The stress of the situation overwhelmed Martha. She often gets a bad rap, but I can relate. She was getting stuff done. Important stuff, like seeing that her guests had something to eat! But the text says, "Martha was distracted by all of the preparations that had to be made." When we get caught up in the vicious cycle of busyness, we are often distracted from the most important things. This is worth taking note of because distractions caused by stress often cause us to miss divine opportunities to connect and go deeper with Jesus. They distort our perspective, and they will at times make us say things we wish we had not said. "Don't you care that my sister has left me to do the work by myself? Tell her to help me!" There will always be things to do, tasks to check off, ministries to lead, but sometimes we have to push the pause button on all those things and just sit with Jesus.

Mary took a moment just to sit at the feet of Jesus. Mary is not excused from doing the work of ministry, but she reminds us that our activity has more focus when it is constantly being fed by Jesus. She reminds us that our commitment to serving must always center on Jesus. This story invites us to consider a balanced life. A life that serves willingly and also one that attends to ways to be in the presence of God. You can't be in the presence of God and worry all the time. You can't be in the presence of God and be stressed all the time. We have to feed our focus. Our relationship with Jesus is our focus. Growing in our understanding of who and whose we are in Christ Jesus is our focus.

Lightly and Freely

Remember that the way of Jesus is to live lightly and freely. The burden is not meant to be heavy or overly burdensome. When Jesus' very presence is our first priority, we can lift our eyes from the long list of tasks to be done and instead focus on their greater purpose. Busyness is not the way of Jesus. Sure, Jesus was always on the move, but he always stopped to be present with someone who called out to him. He saw the people nobody else saw. He heard cries from people others had stopped listening to. He knew how to be present with people, even in the middle of busyness and sometimes chaos. Jesus was a leader who modeled pulling away from the crowd in order to spend time alone with God.

I don't know about you, but I've been guilty of being too caught up in the work of the church and have forgotten to be present with Jesus. I've seen all that needed to be done and knew that "somebody's got to do the work," so I neglected spending time with Jesus in order to get it done. The work of the faith community is not meant to be a heavy burden. If church feels forced and we're all exhausted by it, then I suggest to you that we're not doing it right.

Sometimes it starts at the top with pastors who become the sole caregivers for a community—pastoral care, weddings, funerals, visitations—we take on the burden of everything. I took on everything. But the healthiest thing we can do is teach our people how to care for one another. I don't have to do long-term counseling with someone; I'm not even qualified! So, now I refer people to professionals. Being a pastor doesn't mean that I'm the only one who can visit people, mentor people, teach people the Bible, lead a meeting, or even preach. My job (though it took me a long time to realize it) is to equip and empower my church members to take care of one another. My job is to raise up leaders who can share the leadership load. My job is to keep pointing back to Jesus. My job is to stay close to Jesus and lead from that place.

Worship

As a pastor, I used to worship only as an institutional leader. When I became the General Secretary of Discipleship Ministries, for the first time in many years, I didn't have any weekly worship leadership responsibilities. I just got to go to church and worship. Now that I'm on the other side, I am desperate to get to worship to lay down my burdens. What I've learned by just going to church on Sundays is how vital a worship gathering is for an opportunity to enter into God's presence, to take all the weight of my job and stress and take it to the altar of God. Worship has been like living water to me because it reminds me of who God is. In worship gatherings, we celebrate the presence of God, and we remember that God is bigger than any problem or stress that we have. The key is that we've got to be able to release our worries and give them to God.

As I enter into worship, I don't want to leave the same way I came in. Worship is so significant because it shifts my attitude, my mood. It elevates my thinking and allows me to release emotions. When I leave worship, I feel lighter. I exhale. I am reminded of God's presence in my life, in the midst of all that I'm experiencing. It's vitally important to worship, not as an obligation but as a privilege. I know what David meant in Psalm 122 when he said, "I was glad when they said unto me, / Let us go into the house of the LORD" (v. 1, KJV). I know how desperate he was to connect with God, to remember who God is, to praise him.

Especially when there is so much negativity and stress, and we are overwhelmed by all that's going on in the world, we need to hear the good news over and over and over again. We need to hear the story of God's salvation, grace, mercy, and compassion. We need to be reminded that there's a God who is bigger than whatever I'm going through, who hears and sees and knows my struggle. God's got me. God's going to give me what I need. It's like a cold drink of water. Living Water!

What I have found to be true, both as a leader and as a church member, is that spiritual preparation for worship is essential. We need to get into a head and heart space where we are prepared to hear God's Word and engage in the worship experience. It's my own personal preparation so that I am maximizing my opportunity for deep experience. I set my heart to expect an encounter with God before I walk into worship. This is another intentional act of practicing the presence of God—expecting to encounter God and speaking freely to God.

Soul Reset Practice

I want to invite you to consider all that stresses you out at this very moment. What are you overwhelmed by? Could you make a hard reset and start fresh with a new perspective? What could you do to intentionally practice being with God throughout the course of your days and nights? If you're a pastor or a ministry leader, who are some other leaders in your circle who could share the load? Where can you carve more time to be with your family?

Prayer, worship, practicing the presence of God—these are things that will keep us close to God when we start to feel overwhelmed at the work set before us. Jesus has shown us how to lead and how to care for our souls. He has shown us how to stay close to God, even as he gathered a new community and taught and healed and traveled. Let's lean on Jesus as we go about our lives and ministries and remember that the church doesn't live on our strength alone; it lives only by the power of God. It's not all on us! We can't ruin what God has established, so let's give ourselves a break and remember the unforced rhythms of grace. Let's follow Mary's example of being present with Jesus.

Reflection Questions

1. *Think about the last time you felt stressed or overwhelmed. What words would you use to describe that season?*

2. *Review the story of Mary and Martha. Do you find yourself to be more like Mary, who sees a spiritual moment, or like Martha, who saw only what needed to be accomplished?*

3. *Where do you think your responsibility for another person's spiritual health ends and his or hers begins?*

4. *What do you think it means to practice the presence of God? How can you learn to be open to God's presence with you in every moment of every day?*

5. *When have you felt like "it's all on you"? What are some ways to avoid falling into that trap again and to be sustained by Jesus as the center of your life?*

☼ The daily spiritual practice for this week is **Fasting**. Turn to page 115 to discover ways to practice fasting every day in the coming week.

4

Eat Something

All at once an angel touched him and said, "Get up and eat." He looked around, and there by his head was some bread baked over hot coals, and a jar of water. He ate and drank and then lay down again. The angel of the LORD came back a second time and touched him and said, "Get up and eat, for the journey is too much for you." So he got up and ate and drank. Strengthened by that food, he traveled forty days and forty nights until he reached Horeb, the mountain of God. There he went into a cave and spent the night.

—1 Kings 19:5-9

What are you doing here? Have you ever asked yourself this question? If there was ever a time for us seriously to consider what it means to experience genuine and authentic renewal in our lives, then it is such a time as this. In an essay entitled "The Paradox of Our Age" from his book *Words Aptly Spoken* (Overlake Christian Bookstore, 1995; pp. 197–98), Dr. Bob Moorehead put it like this:

> We've learned how to make a living but not a life; we've added years to life, not life to years. We've cleaned up the air, but polluted the soul; we've split the atom, but not our prejudice; we . . . plan more but accomplish less . . . we learned to rush, but not to wait. . . . These are the days of . . . quick trips, disposable diapers . . . throwaway morality, one-night stands . . . and pills that do everything from cheer, to prevent, quiet or kill. It is a time when there is much in the show window and nothing in the stock room.

We have become a world that is addicted to hurry. Hurry is an emotional pusher. We drive fast when we have plenty of time to get to our destination. We microwave our food even though it tastes better warmed the way it was cooked. We grow impatient waiting in lines when we have no other place to be at that moment. We have to give ourselves permission to slow down. We need to seriously consider and ponder how to receive genuine and authentic renewal in our lives. We need a soul reset.

I love the way the Reverend Dr. Otis McMillan tells the story of an old, retired racing dog. It's a story that's printed in a Fred Craddock book, and lots of pastors have a version of this story, but Dr. McMillan helped me see the parable from a different angle. He tells the story of interviewing a retired greyhound dog. The greyhound was sitting, relaxing, chilling under a tree, sipping on some lemonade. Dr. McMillan asked this greyhound dog, "Why are you just relaxing over there? Shouldn't you be running over at the greyhound track?" And the greyhound dog began to testify. He said, "I've been running for the last three years. I was first out of the box, chasing after that rabbit. I won medal after medal, trophy after trophy, and I expended a whole lot of energy trying to win the race, but I want you to know a couple of days ago I got up before the break of dawn, and I crept out to where the rabbit was kept. And after I peeked into the box, I gave up chasing rabbits. You see although the rabbit *moved*, that rabbit ain't *real*."

We've been chasing after rabbits, but the rabbit is not real. My mission, as I speak and travel and even in writing this book, is to remind you, and me, that "the rabbit is not real." In other words, we are spinning our wheels and chasing our tails until we're exhausted and burned out. We are living life on the fast track. But I have discovered that the fast track is really a treadmill. Success is an illusion if it is not defined by the values of our faith. Success will make you feel overly responsible if it is not grounded in your faith.

In the story of Elijah (1 Kings 19), we see a man who, in the literal sense, is emotionally, spiritually, and physically drained. The irony of the story is that Elijah had just experienced the greatest success of his life: He had declared a drought in order to punish the Israelite nation for its idolatry, the worship of Baal, which had been encouraged by the queen, Jezebel. The drought had ended in a contest between Elijah and the prophets of Baal, and a God who would answer his prophet's call from heaven would be vindicated as the one true God. Elijah won the contest! But now he was on the run, fleeing to Beersheba to escape the wrath of Jezebel. Elijah had been on the mountaintop with God, and he had accomplished a great deal in ministry, but now he was running for his life. He walks out into the desert and sits down by a large bush, and in a state of spiritual and emotional exhaustion, he now asks God to "just let me die."

Can you relate to that? If we were honest, more people than we know have been exactly where Elijah is in this moment. But can we be real enough with one another to be that honest? Can we begin to build faith communities that can speak truth to one another? Exhaustion and burnout are rampant in church today. Church leaders and pastors are burning out at alarming rates. People are quitting ministries and pulpits because they are exhausted and have lost passion for their work. The truth is that life wears down even the best of us. Sometimes we arrive at these places in life not because of failure but because we didn't manage our success well.

Tests and Trials

All of us experience trying times and tests in our lives, and I believe these times are necessary for our growth because they test the courage of our convictions and the depth of our faith. We can always be sure that the same God who led us in is the same God who will lead us out. Trouble is a platform for the display of God's almighty grace and power in our lives. For Elijah, things looked worse than they really were. External circumstances seemed overwhelming, but he was never out of the care of an almighty God. God didn't scold Elijah for feeling down, but God did give him a new perspective. God sent an angel to arrange for a much-needed vacation. Elijah got all the food he needed. He got all the rest he needed. He got all the reflection time he needed. Sometimes that's God's call to us: *Rest and renew.*

Rest to Reset

When we think about renewal, we have to remember the power of sabbath, that observing a sabbath is one of the ways God renews us. Sabbath means stopping and resting; it is a gift from our Creator God. The truth of the matter is we sometimes get so caught up in trying to change the world—transforming the world, a worthy mission—that we keep going and going and going. Pretty soon we are no longer operating under the power of God, and we begin to try to operate out of our own strength. We forget that this is spiritual warfare that we're dealing with because our struggle is not against flesh and blood but against the spiritual forces of evil.

Would you agree that life wears down even the best of us sometimes? If we allow our jobs and activities to work us into an early grave, then they will. God knew about the need to rest, finishing the work of Creation and then resting. God blessed the seventh day and called it special. What made it special? Rest. An intentional, set-apart time to rest from work and to rest in God's love is essential to a soul reset. We've got to stop the hustle in order to let our hearts, bodies, and minds reset.

Jesus knew how to rest, and he invited us into his rest when he said, "Come to Me, all you who labor and are heavy laden, and I will give you rest" (Matt. 11:28-30, NKJV). He didn't say, "Come and let me give you a bunch of work to do." He didn't say, "Follow me and you will have to-do lists like you've never seen before." No, Jesus said he gives us *rest*—rest for our whole selves. Remember that God's salvation is for our whole selves: God cares about our bodies, our minds, and our souls. Sabbath rest is a must for a soul reset. It is an essential ingredient for spiritual, emotional, and physical renewal.

A rested body will energize your life. A rested mind is capable of creative thinking. Our spirits need time to reconnect to the source of our identity as children of God. We need to create the time, space, and rest to remember who and whose we are. We need those sabbath times to remember that church isn't something we do only on Sundays; it's who we are as Christ followers. The apostle Paul says that it is in Christ that "I live and move and have my being" (Acts 17:28, adapted).

God gave Elijah rest for the journey that lay ahead of him and told him to eat something. Elijah needed some rest and some food in order to get back to the work set before him. Sometimes God will have to attend to our physical needs before encountering us. Sometimes we are not ready to receive what God has in store for us because we are just too worn out. God cared about Elijah's physical well-being *and* his spiritual well-being:

> So he got up and ate and drank. Strengthened by that
> food, he traveled forty days and forty nights until he
> reached Horeb, the mountain of God. There he went

into a cave and spent the night. And the word of the
LORD came to him: "What are you doing here, Elijah?"

(1 Kings 19:8-9)

It's amazing how many new possibilities emerge after a day of rest and renewal in the presence of God. Fortunately for Elijah, things looked worse than they really were. When we are tired and fatigued, our perspective on our situation is often distorted. Our sense of doom is magnified. God gave Elijah a new perspective. God sent an angel to arrange for a much-needed vacation. Elijah ate food and rested. He had time for reflection. God gave Elijah rest for the journey that lay ahead of him. God cared about both his physical well-being and his spiritual well-being.

"What Are You Doing Here?"

Sabbath rest is important for a soul reset because it clears space for self-inspection. God knew what Elijah was doing, but God asked anyway so that Elijah could begin to rethink his situation with a new perspective.

And Elijah didn't get far before he needed to reset again. This time he hid in a cave, waiting to hear from God, until God came to him and asked what he was doing there (see 1 Kings 19:9-13). Of course, once again God knew what Elijah was doing, but God asked anyway so that Elijah could begin to assess his situation more deeply. God was saying to Elijah, "I didn't save you to be in this condition, Elijah. What are you doing here in a cave on Mount Horeb? Didn't I send you to preach to my people in Israel? Shouldn't you be leading my people in a great revival? I didn't call you to run and hide away in a cave. I called you to stand before kings, to defy false gods and prophets, and to be an example of righteousness for the people of Israel. So, Elijah . . . what are you doing here?" It was a call for Elijah to examine his life. It was a call for Elijah to reorder his priorities. It was a call for Elijah to ask the tough questions.

What questions is God asking you about what God's trying to do in and through you? There are a lot of reasons we could be in a "cave." It could be a divorce, an abusive situation, a financial disaster. It could be ministry itself or it could be broken dreams. In order to lead effectively, we must be maturing in our faith, and that requires time to confront ourselves about where we are in life. The result is often a reordering of our priorities.

It's interesting to me that Elijah comes to the place called the "Mountain of God," and there at the Mountain of God he finds a cave. This mountain was a place of great significance for the people of Israel. It was here that God had met Moses in a burning bush. It was here that Moses had received the Ten Commandments from God. This is the place you would expect to be enveloped in the presence of God. But here, Elijah found a cave.

During a really exhausting season of ministry while I was pastoring Saint Mark UMC in Wichita, Kansas, I attended a national conference on preaching. There was nothing wrong in our ministry. In fact, we were experiencing a period of sustained growth. But I was tired, and my intent was simply to be renewed. I spent three days at this conference listening to some of the most gifted and anointed preachers in the country. The worship experiences were Spirit-filled and were attended by about 2,000 persons each evening. The music was good. People were clapping and raising their hands. But I remember being in that space one evening and feeling as if God were a million miles away. That moment was a sobering reminder to me that my renewal time had to include some time for self-inspection and reflection.

Soul Reset Practice

Just like Elijah, we need some self-inspection time. Not only do we need a sabbath, we need a soul inspection. Perhaps we are here because we did not manage success well. Sure, we've got all the marks of success: We've got the reputation; we've got the title. But success is a dangerous illusion. Elijah says in 1 Kings 19:10, "I am the only one left." Success has the tendency to make you feel overly responsible, like everything rides on your strength and your strength alone. But in sabbath, we lean into *God's* strength and remember that God can do what God is going to do, with or without us. Participating in God's work is God's gift to us, not a burden to bear.

What are you doing here? is a question I now ask myself regularly. I have developed a new habit called "on-the-balcony." This is what I call the time that I set aside at least once a quarter to reflect and ask myself the tough questions in order to avoid the cave. It's a time to take a 30,000-foot look at my ministry and my life. It gives me time with God and time to be reminded that Jesus is in control of my life. It gives me time to try and avoid the traps of burnout and exhaustion. I have discovered that while I cannot avoid difficult circumstances, I can change how I respond to them. Even in my "cave" experiences, I am convinced that the God who brought me there is the same God who will lead me out. I believe trying times and challenges in our lives are necessary because they test the courage of our convictions and the depth of our faith. We can't have a testimony without a test. We can't know God as a problem-solver if we never have any problems. Our most difficult moments provide a platform for the display of God's grace and power in our lives.

Take a few minutes now for self-inspection. What are you doing here, right now, at this point in your life? Are you exhausted? burned out? in need of sabbath? Assess the state of your soul, and ask God to help you reset and begin again with fresh energy and strength for the journey.

Reflection Questions

1. *What practices help you avoid burnout and exhaustion and live a centered, whole life? Do you have a regular sabbath practice? What does your sabbath look like?*

2. *What are some of your mountaintop moments? When have you experienced times when your soul felt you were hiding in a cave, afraid and waiting to hear from God?*

3. *How do tests and trials teach you about who God is and who you are?*

4. *What is the 30,000-foot view of your life right now? What can you learn from looking at your life this way?*

⏻ The daily spiritual practice for this week is **Taking Care of Your Body**. Turn to page 118 to discover ways to practice taking care of your body every day in the coming week.

Life in Crisis

*"My eyes have grown dim with grief;
my whole frame is but a shadow."*

—Job 17:7

The year of 2012 was my year of extreme grief. After years of fighting my way back to healing from depression and breakdown in California, I was thrown right back into the pit. In February 2012, my mom died after having survived a brain aneurysm, cancer, and the rehabilitation that followed. The paramedics had thought she was having an asthma attack, but it was really a heart attack. My brother called me from the hospital and told me that the ambulance had come to get our mother. She had not been breathing. I could hear the machines and cries over the phone. I heard the cries of my brother and my sister-in-law. I could hear the frenzy of people in the room trying to resuscitate my mom for the third time. I told my brother to put the doctor on the phone, and in a moment that haunts me to this day, I told the doctor to let her go. My mom and I had talked about her last wishes and the Do Not Resuscitate question. My sense was that she was ready to go.

In that moment, I was in my living room, holding the telephone, and I just let her go . . . and a few moments later, my brother said she was gone. I fell onto the floor, sobbing. I had never felt anything like that before in my life. The grief was immediate. My wife and kids ran into the room and found me in a depth of pain that I had never felt, ever. But like a good minister, I gathered myself and went into pastor mode. I preached my mother's funeral and was strong for everyone, until I wasn't. In the next few months, I fell apart. I went into a depth of depression that I had never experienced. I honestly did not think I would come out of it; I didn't think I would make it. I had been off medication, but knew I had to go back on it. I needed help and counseling. Because I hadn't completely learned my lesson, I continued working, pastoring, trying to hold things together at church and home. But on the inside, I was torn apart. I was a mess.

Soon after my mom died, my brother called and said he had something to share with me. He told me that the person I had thought was my father was actually not my father. *What?* The man I thought was my father . . . *wasn't?* You can imagine, that hit me like a ton of bricks. Another piece of my reality, my normal, had been ripped from my life. It was a loss. I lost part of my identity, and it was painful because I had to have hard conversations with my dad that included DNA tests. When the results came in the mail a few weeks later, I learned with certainty that the man I thought was my father was, in fact, not.

I was already out of emotional capacity, so grief hit hard and showed no mercy.

My *Job-like* season continued into August of that year (still 2012), when my brother died of a heart attack. Two weeks later, I lost my grandmother. About a month after that, I lost one of my best friends from high school. It's hard to imagine that so much loss could happen in such a short time, but there I was, neck-deep in devastation, wondering why all this pain was coming at me. I didn't have time to grieve properly from one loss to the next. Sadly, I hadn't learned a lesson from previous dark seasons and didn't take any time off. I thought maybe if I powered through and just kept working, I'd find a way to be okay. I thought being a good leader meant stuffing down my pain, stress, and heartbreak. I thought I needed to put on a mask and push through my feelings. That would prove to be a huge mistake.

By November 2012, my panic attacks were back, or so I thought. Randomly, I would begin to shake uncontrollably and lose my breath. Just walking from my office to my car made me short of breath. Then I noticed a pain in my leg. On the way to a retreat, I called my doctor and told him what was happening, and he told me to go to the emergency room immediately. He didn't say why; he just said to hang up the phone and go. It turns out that I had two pulmonary embolisms—a clot in both of my lungs and in my left leg. I was literally on the verge of death. The doctors could not believe that I was sitting there alive. They said I was so lucky. I was lying in the hospital room on my bed, flat on my back, and that's what it took to get me to slow down long enough to get in touch with my grief. It was just right there, under the surface, waiting to be dealt with.

In those first moments after I received the news that I had escaped death, I was working it out in my head how I'd get to church to preach by Sunday. Because life comes at you and doesn't really care if it's a convenient time, we had a lot going on at the church that I needed to take care of. We were in the middle of the capital campaign, and it was Commitment Sunday. This was the conclusion of months of planning, meetings, gatherings, and sharing vision with the entire church. I was thinking, *Wow, really, God? Now? In the middle of an important season at church, you've got me laid out in an emergency room?*

But now I look back and see that God was saying to me during this time, "Junius, you are so hardheaded. The capital campaign is not the most important thing in your life. Your walk with me is the most important, and you need time to grieve. You need to take care of yourself. You're going to stop everything and reset." That was the most pivotal turning point in my spiritual journey and in my leadership journey. That was the moment when I knew I was in for another soul reset. Everything was out of alignment. My body wasn't healthy. My spirit was like a desert. My mind wasn't in a good place. God made it clear to me that I needed to start again. So many moments that year, I wanted to give up. I was in a dark place. There were so many days when I literally just tried to force myself out of the darkness.

I did not make it to church to preach that Sunday. I was in the hospital for a week while my body healed. I had deep and difficult conversations with my wife. I remember she said she would not know what to do if something ever happened to me. I could see that she was worried, but I assured her that there was a plan. However, we were talking about two different plans: I was talking about the crisis plan for our church, while she was talking about our relationship. She meant that she didn't know what she'd do without me. Talk about a wakeup call! That's how badly I needed a reset. Not only were my body, mind, and spirit in need of a reset but also I needed to tend to my relationship with my family.

My Conversations with God

That week in the hospital, I had an open dialogue with God. *Haven't I been through enough, God? I'm just trying to be faithful and do what I'm called to do, Lord. Why would you allow this to happen?*

This experience was a wakeup call. God showed me that I was so out of focus on so many levels. It was an opportunity for me to reflect on my life that could have happened only with me lying in a hospital bed. I never would have stopped working long enough to reflect on or deal with my grief over the year. Finally, there was time for me to be in deep, deep, deep prayer. Also, it was an opportunity to be reminded that if I were gone, that church would keep rolling because Sunday still happened. I watched the worship service online that Sunday, and it was a really good service!

This hospital stay was a turning point. It was the beginning of me saying, *God, I need you to walk with me through my pain and my suffering.* Just as I walk with other people when they walk through trials, this was God saying to me, "You need to let me walk with you, and you need to let other people walk with you through this." I began to open up more about my grief and depression. Before, I never would have talked to my church about what was going on in my head and my heart. Somehow, I thought this was different. I felt like the way to make it past my grief was to work my way through it. The problem had been that in the midst of my grief, I hadn't taken time to feel. I had always projected okay-ness; it was always about projecting strength as a leader. I had to be strong. But I was dying on the inside, and what I most needed was to be able to process that with some people who love me. I needed to share with my people that I'm not totally okay. I'm not a robot or a machine. I'm not a person who doesn't feel things. Here was God, telling me, "If you're going to do this, this is how you're going to have to move going forward." It's like a lesson learned *again*: "You didn't quite learn the lesson the first time, so let's try again."

Job

Life got real for me, just like it got real for Job. Job cried out to God in the midst of his pain. I learned to cry out to God too. *I need you, God. I need you.* It was so personal. I wasn't crying out to God for help with a budget or a church need—*I* needed God. I was fighting for my life. I was fighting for a desire to still be alive. I needed to feel held by God.

As I began to cry out to God, I began to lean into the promise that God could be trusted. I didn't see wholeness right in front of me or the path I would take to get there, but I knew that I had to trust God. That was my no-matter-what moment with God. That was my "yet praise" moment with God. That was my thankful-for-life moment with God. So many times that year, I felt like I'd be okay with not living anymore. But there, in that moment, I gave my life back to God, for whatever life God had in store for me; and the power that God gives me, I'm going to operate out of that.

I wasn't immediately whole in that moment. I had a long road ahead of me. I had work to do. But the work wouldn't be about adding tasks and plans; it would be about hearing God's voice anew, with a freshness and power. My grief had shut me down emotionally like a defense mechanism. It was so overwhelming I didn't know what to do with it. Setting off in a new way would mean giving God my grief. This would be the start of a new chapter in my walk with God. This time, I would be learning to walk in the unforced rhythms of grace that Jesus invites us into. This time, I would learn what walking lightly and freely with Jesus really means.

Why, God?

Job comes face-to-face with grief, suffering, and loss. It's not sugarcoated or glossed over. It's a raw reality. Job is a wealthy man, has a great family, runs a great business, has a great reputation; he is humble before God—all the things we would aspire to. Yet in an instant, he comes face-to-face with a different reality. So how do we handle it when unexpected storms come into our lives? When we experience unbelievable loss? Job lost every-thing—family, business, employees. It just kept coming, like my experiences in 2012. What do we do when the grief just keeps on coming? Where is God in all this?

How do you maintain faith in the face of the problems and contradictions that the world produces for our faith? That's what Job's dilemma is all about. Sometimes our suffering is out of our control. Sometimes we deal with things of our own doing. Sometimes we deal with other people. The question is, how do we handle it? To live an abundant life doesn't mean we won't face trouble or storms, or that everything will always be good times, safety, health, and wealth. It just means we have the capacity to deal with things as they come.

The story of Job is really about a response. Job's response to his suffering was to worship. We go to church on Sundays and it's a ritual: Let's sing some songs and pray, hear the message, and then go home and eat the roast. That's not what Job did. His was not an ignoring-my-reality worship. It was raw worship. It was a gut-wrenching laying yourself before God. That's what Job did. He said, "God, you're in this. Despite what I'm experiencing right now, it does not diminish my faith in you." That was Job's wor-ship. In the midst of his pain, he was crying out to God, declar-ing that God was in the middle of this pain. Job couldn't explain it or understand it, but he was going to bless the Lord.

I've discovered firsthand that you've got to fight for a mindset like that. You've got to fight for it by worshiping and by praying and by being in community, by being in authentic relationships and being vulnerable with others. That's fighting for the faith you have in God. It's risking rejection. It's risking people saying to you, "Get over it." It's risking people telling you it's not that bad.

Jesus is the ultimate example. He entered into our pain and rejection and took it on himself so that we would have the capacity through his power to experience suffering with him. When we go through grief, we get a better understanding that we receive good things from the hands of God. Every now and then there will be tears and trials, but the scripture declares that weeping only lasts the night and joy comes in the morning.

Good Friends and the Right Voices

At first, Job's friends got it right. They came and sat with Job in his grief. But when the grief got too heavy, they felt they had to say something. I pastored a family who lost a son suddenly. The parents had been on a cruise, so I met the son's sister at the hospital to be there when their parents arrived. I knew what was coming, and I knew it was going to be unbelievable grief. That is exactly what happened. The mom came in and was broken, sobbing, holding on to her dead son. We stood in that room, silent except for the sound of sobbing. This woman didn't need me to say anything or try to make any sense out of the senseless pain. The best thing I could offer her family was presence. There aren't any words that can comfort in these moments. We don't have to say things when we walk with people through grief. We can offer silence and presence, not judgment or advice.

Job's friends started out offering presence, but when the hits kept coming, they lost their cool. They couldn't just sit with Job anymore without offering opinions or advice. Somehow, they decided it would be a good idea to ask Job what he had done to receive such wrath from God! It should come as no surprise that I heard some of those same rumblings from people in my city during my year of grief. People do not know what to say to grieving folks, do they?

Even Job's wife had weird advice. She suggested that he curse God so that Job could just die and be put out of his misery. I'd like to give her the benefit of the doubt that maybe, just maybe, she was saying she didn't want to see him suffer anymore. Job's wife was looking at this man's suffering and didn't know how to process it, so she was just guessing at what to say or do.

But Job's choice was to live and to trust God, no matter what. Job was going to hold on, no matter what came at him. Loss comes in different forms—losing a job, going through a divorce, or facing a financial setback. People walk around all day, every day, going through things we have no idea about. When we do get an invitation to witness someone's grief or loss, we've got to learn that we can't solve the problems. We don't have to have answers or solutions. We don't have to give advice. What we can do is just be present with hurting people, right where they are. We can assure them of God's presence in their lives, even in the midst of what they're going through.

My assessment of Job's life is that one week he's encouraged and doing great, and the next he's on the verge of a nervous breakdown. I can so relate to that trajectory. How do we respond to adversity? That is the journey we are on as followers of Jesus. At the beginning, Job can bounce back and worship. But later, he's in a pit and can't make sense of anything at all. In the pit, Job just looks for God. Let's all remember that God can handle our raw emotion, our complaints, our discouragements, our anger, and our questions.

God Restores

As I began to climb out of my grief, restoration came to my life in a tremendous way. God said, "Even in the midst of your loss, I'm going to birth a new thing in you." I remember sharing with my church that the capital campaign we were in was a faith walk with God. It wasn't about debt reduction or funding a children's wing. It was about our walk with God, our faith, and what that looks like lived out in our community. I earnestly believe that when we walk closely with God, he will birth new things that we can't even imagine. As I was still journeying through grief and preaching through a capital campaign, God surprised us in January of 2013. We got the opportunity to start a second campus, which we hadn't ever dreamed of happening in the midst of a campaign.

So, this new thing, this new vision, came out of the darkest period of my life, and it really helped me to reengage and dream. It brought back unspeakable joy. It brought back purpose and excitement, all restored a hundredfold: New people would come to know Christ and experience the love of God. It deepened my testimony and my story. It even changed my approach to preaching. The first sermon on the new campus wasn't about the church's growth; it was about the power of God to resurrect, to bring life to dry bones, to help us overcome. I told my story that first Sunday of this new church, and it set a tone for that campus from the beginning that we'd be a church who told the truth about what's going on in our lives. One woman greeted me after the service that day, and her excitement wasn't about the new church or the worship celebration; she was elated that I would share my imperfection on Launch Sunday! The campus started attracting people who were willing to be vulnerable and live and minister authentically. It's a unique and special place. My personal growth led me to share my story, and in my sharing, our church grew in ways I couldn't have imagined. I never would have talked about myself like that, but I felt the Spirit lead me to a new kind of ministry.

I have learned that faith in God is a journey, not a destination. Even as I live with hope and God is bringing light into darkness, I still have bad days. Part of my journey is learning when I need to push through and when I need to rest. Soon after our new church had begun, there was a day where the newspaper came to do a feature story on our new campus. Because bad days don't announce themselves ahead of time, this happened on a really bad day for me. I knew I was struggling, and I was not looking forward to this interview. My communications staff person hadn't heard from me yet, so she called me at home and asked me where I was. I told her I was having a hard day and that I wasn't going to make it there. But she told me to get up and get dressed and come to the church for this interview.

It took all I had to get there. I finally made it, and I told the reporter about how God had given birth to this new thing and it was amazing. He took some pictures of me in the sanctuary, and I can tell you with certainty that the smile on my face in that photo did not tell the whole story of what was going on inside me. When I look at the photo, I can tell you exactly what was going on in my heart that day. The headline of the story was about newness and a new, exciting church. The picture of me looks great on the outside: I'm smiling in the sanctuary of our growing, dynamic church. But inside, I'm having a super-dark day, still reeling from a year of suffering and grief. God is still working on us and through us, even in our dark days. I look at that picture and think, *Man, I was on a journey then—not at all arrived, but God was still using me.*

The Power of Honest Community

Part of my healing process was learning to be authentic and being open with my story and learning to lead by example in the way of vulnerability. So, in a 3,000-member church, with what seemed like a million different ministries, I decided to gather and teach a small group of men we called a fraternity. In our first gathering as a new small group, I shared my story of discovering the truth about my father. When I shared that story, it created a space that I had never experienced before in church. It created a space of authenticity and openness. Other men began to tell their stories. Grown men were weeping, sharing a similar story for the first time in their lives. It was amazing to me, and it was clear to me that this was not going to be an ordinary Bible study—this was going to be a journey with God that led to freedom. I discovered that vulnerability would be one of the keys to unlock a path to deeper relationship with God and with one another.

Soul Reset Practice

One song that gets me through hard days is called "Journey On," by Elms District. The words inspire me and remind me to approach each challenge with hope: "You've only got one more river to cross . . . And you're on the other side." Day by day, one river at a time, one storm at a time, one mountain at a time, we learn to practice depending upon God for strength. We learn to praise God in the storm, through the storm, and for getting us to the other side of the storm.

Some things to take with you on the journey to healing are simplicity, reexamination of priorities, time to grieve, worship, and tending to relationships. We've got to clear away clutter and unimportant things in our lives in order to get through our grief. We've got to reexamine our priorities and make sure that we have enough margin to do the work of healing. We've got to take the space we need to grieve and not rush through it. We've got to discover worship as an antidote to despair, to reclaim our lives with God as the center. The practice of worship is where we reset. We've got to remember and tend to all of the important people in our lives and nurture those relationships. Tell your family and friends that you love them, and thank them for walking with you through your journey. Trust that as you walk every day with God, grief will get just a little bit better.

I want to invite you to worship God. Turn on some worship music right now and sing along. Whatever you're doing, however you're feeling, lift up your heart to God in worship for a few minutes. Let worship work in your soul and reset your heart.

Reflection Questions

1. *What are some moments of grief or loss that you have faced in your life?*

2. *Do you feel like you have to project a sense of being "okay" to the world? If so, why?*

3. *What did Job's friends do right? What did they do wrong? How can your community be one that allows mystery, vulnerability, and authenticity when tragic loss occurs?*

4. *How have small groups helped you grow as a follower of Jesus? What are you personally looking for in a small group?*

5. *How can worship help you reset your soul?*

⏻ The daily spiritual practice for this week is **Worship**. Turn to page 121 to discover ways to practice worship every day in the coming week.

6

Living in the Light

For God did not send his Son into the world to condemn the world, but to save the world through him.

—John 3:17

One of the things you learn from an early age in the church is John 3:16: "For God so loved the world that he gave his one and only Son, that whoever believes in him shall not perish but have eternal life." We've emphasized memorizing that one verse as a description of what it means to be saved by Jesus Christ. But if we read ahead just one more verse, we discover that following Jesus means much more than just being saved for heaven someday in the future. The very next verse tells even more about the character of God—God didn't come to condemn us but to save us. God didn't come to shame us into relationship. God didn't send Jesus to condemn us and make us run and hide. No, Jesus came to free us from shame and fear and sin and darkness.

I've discovered that the antidote to fear and shame is vulnerability. We need to talk more about our failures. It seems ironic, but people learn more from our failures than our successes. If I'm in a conversation with young pastors, they may look up to me because of the success of my ministry or because I'm speaking on a national stage—that has some type of draw or allure to it. But it's more helpful for me to say, "Let me tell you about the time when I stood up to speak, and I didn't even make it to first base! Let me tell you about the time I was at the hotel, and it took everything in me just to walk out the door to go get on that stage. Let me tell you about being so overwhelmed by life that just trying to prepare to speak became a grinding task and was so difficult." As I am talking about success and things we did well in our church plant, I am also learning to tell both sides of the stories, including the downside—the things we tried that didn't work or something that turned out to be a really bad investment in ministry. That way, people get a clearer picture of their own capacity to risk, to fail, and to try again. People have to hear both sides of the story to connect with that.

Hidden Pain

During my years as a pastor in Wichita, Kansas, I sat on a board of directors with a prominent businessman. We became friends and would share stories about where we had seen God moving and other faith issues. I never would have guessed that he was in any kind of pain. I had no clue that he was struggling with depression, no clue that he was struggling with his sense of self-image—the pressures of being a successful leader in the community. I don't know all the circumstances, but when I got news of his suicide, it sent a shockwave through my spirit. I couldn't believe it. I had just seen him a few days before. We had talked about our families. The thought haunted me that I could be in a "normal" conversation with someone and he could be so good at hiding his pain that literally, within hours, he could take his life. We get really good at hiding our pain and presenting a version of ourselves we think people want to see day to day.

Immediately, I began talking to my church about what it means to be transparent and vulnerable together in our community. I was so troubled by this suicide that I began thinking about my approach to ministry and the authenticity of our community. It was like a red flag or a clarion call to say, "We need to be having these conversations on a regular basis." How do we live in community? How do we ensure that people feel safe to share their pain in our community?

It hit me that this man's suicide affected not only his family but also the church because he was known as a faith leader in the community. It had a profound effect on people who were not even in the faith community. The irony is that we falsely believe things that happen to leaders in the church don't affect people outside the church. But people outside the church have a healthy respect for leaders in the church and the witness of the church. When things like this happen, we're reminded of the power of our witness in the community. These are moments when we can be open and transparent.

At his funeral, there was not a single word said about suicide. I can only assume the reason why is because of the shame and the stigma around it. People have their own beliefs about what happens when you take your own life. But if there's ever a time to talk about that issue, it would have been in that setting. People were there from all over, from inside and outside the church.

Another funeral I attended was a stark contrast. Pastor Adam Hamilton gave a sermon at the funeral of a young man who had died by suicide. Adam gave a celebration of his life, but he also named the struggle, how a good kid had been in a battle he couldn't overcome. This was the one struggle he couldn't fight. He had called his mom the day of the suicide, proving that in our most fragile, hopeless moments, we still reach out and yearn to connect with someone. Adam offered the ministry of the church to those who might be struggling at that moment. He gave three invitations—an invitation into community, an invitation for people who might be struggling with suicide, and an invitation for loved ones and caregivers who need support. That's connecting the ministry of the church in a very real, practical way when people are walking through your doors asking, "Why?" Though we can't answer the *why* question, we can answer the *what* question. What can help us draw closer to God in these moments? What can enlarge our sense of who God is in these moments? As we embrace that, it's an opportunity for a whole community to go deeper together into relationships and into our walk with God.

Saying No to Shame

Secrets have power only because they're secrets. The only way to take away the power of a secret is to speak it into community, so we've got to find creative ways to invite people into vulnerability. After the US economy crashed in 2008–2009, I had a lot of businesspersons in my church who were negatively affected by it. One couple left the church because they were ashamed that their business was failing. People had seen them in a certain way, they felt, and they couldn't deal with what people might think of them there.

Shame can shut us down. It's a paradox: One would think that in the church you should be able to experience failures and losses and still be loved. But the church has become so success- and image-driven that our people can't just be themselves—failures and triumphs together. In the midst of our failures, we sometimes need to be reminded that we are still loved.

In the Gospel of Matthew (26:33-34), Jesus' disciple Peter confidently promises Jesus that he would never desert him. Jesus responds by telling Peter, "This very night, before the rooster crows, you will disown me three times." And following this, Peter does in fact deny knowing or being associated with Jesus three times. The next thing Peter knew, Jesus was being beaten and killed. Can you imagine the utter shame Peter felt after he heard that rooster crow? I imagine that it must have been pretty difficult for him to carry such shame and self-loathing in those following hours.

But Jesus comes to Peter in one of his Resurrection appearances (John 21) and says to him, "Do you love me? Feed my sheep." This is a reminder that somehow in those moments of deep shame, we can still hear Jesus saying, "You're my child. I still have vision for your life. Feed my sheep." It's in those moments on the discipleship journey that with those habitual practices, the spiritual disciplines, we discover their full value. This is because we have the capacity to draw back to memory. We have the capacity to hear the still, small voice of Jesus in our darkest moments. You can go from, "I want to die today" to a voice that whispers back, *You don't have to die today*." That's the story of life and where a lot of people find themselves.

I was talking to a young man recently who had just lost his mom. He said he wanted to die. I said, "Man, what are you feeling?" He told me he felt like his world was over, that he could have done more, that he had failed his mom. He's a musician, and he said he has even felt like he had heard God's voice when he's playing music. He said he can't keep going. But in those moments of grief, you have capacity and strength you never knew you had. I've learned from experience that spiritual disciplines and practices prepare us for the unimaginable. We have a steady ground and a depth of capacity to keep going when we thought we couldn't go on. That's what the practices do—they keep us connected to our Source.

Peter and Judas

In the events leading up to Jesus' crucifixion, Peter and Judas both betrayed Jesus and found themselves ashamed of what they had done. For Judas, his shame was centered on an act of betrayal. He betrayed Jesus. His act of betrayal led him to shame. He could not reconcile his relationship with God with his betrayal, and in shame, he took his own life.

The number-one cause of stress is living inconsistently with your own self-values. At the heart of it, it's a betrayal of that which we say we believe. It's when we betray our faith—when we don't take a stand, when we act in ways that are contrary to the ways of Jesus, when we make our own personal mistakes. These things are cumulative; they add up over time and lead to an impending sense of *I can't get past this*. That's when we have to receive the grace of God in our lives. Judas could have gone a different way. He could have listened for God's voice and asked for Jesus' forgiveness.

Peter took his shame and dealt with it in community. He went out in a boat with his friends. By morning, Peter was reunited with Jesus, having breakfast with him and being invited into a life of carrying on Jesus' ministry. Judas took his shame into isolation and into the dark of night. Peter saw the light break through in the morning, a light that would pierce through the shame and give the mercy a new morning brings.

There are two responses to shame we can have as leaders and as Jesus followers: Isolate or move into community. It's easy to have a bad meeting or a bad day and want to go and hide. But we have to push past that and get our people around us. We have to confess that we are broken people and we need grace and mercy, and a reminder that we are loved, forgiven, and free.

Isolation is often what I turn to. I am learning to be fully conscious of when I want to isolate and turn inward. When something doesn't go the way I wanted it to go, I don't want to be with people asking me about it; I'd rather go and hide. That's a sign of shame and an indication I might be going down a road that might not end well.

The opposite of that is to find community, to have a small group and to be open and transparent with them. In the midst of the group, you are able to say what you're feeling, get help processing, or even just be with people who will sit with you and remind you that all shall be well. I have a group of brothers who are helping me live into this spiritual practice. We live in different parts of the country, and we meet in person a few times a year. But at any given moment, any one of us can ask for a conference call to help process difficult moments or to celebrate something significant happening in our lives.

Peter ends up on the beach with Jesus. He transforms his worst day into a reminder of call. God still loves you and has a purpose for you—"Go feed my sheep." Judas transforms his worst day by taking his own life. The truth and reality is, all of us can have a day like that. We all have a "worst day ever." What are we going to do with it? What is our next step?

The Next Right Step

What do we learn from experiences of suicide in our communities? How do we process that in our churches? It seems like it happens way too often. We have to speak honestly about suicide. It takes the shame out of it. The family feels shame, and people who are experiencing suicidal thoughts are feeling shame. We also have to name that we've all had days that felt too heavy and when we've felt the depth of despair. Sadly, we can too quickly move to judgment: *How could they do that? How could they leave their [kids, spouse, family, friends] like that?* Remind people of the significance of community and of being part of a small group where there is honest sharing and accountability. Small groups are a spiritual practice that is vitally important *koinonia*—soul to soul fellowship—deeper than a potluck. We need that safe community that allows for vulnerability and authentic space to be real. We need a place to confess what's going on in our hearts and our lives, a place to confess what we are struggling with and how deeply we need the grace and mercy of God.

> Have mercy on me, O God,
> according to your unfailing love;
> according to your great compassion
> blot out my transgressions.
> Wash away all my iniquity
> and cleanse me from my sin.
> (Ps. 51:1-2)

Soul Reset Practice

Confession is a lost art in the Protestant church. When was the last time you heard someone talk about confessing our sins? We don't want to talk about that! The scripture declares that if we confess our sins and struggles, then God is faithful to forgive and heal. To confess means to acknowledge that we are not perfect, that sin still exists in our lives—that there are things we do and attitudes we take that keep us from being perfected in love. Confession is important to health, healing, and releasing shame, despondency, depression, and discouragement. Just to confess it, to open your mouth and say, "God, this is where I am," and to have one other person in the world you can just call up and say, "Hey, I just have some things I need to confess. . . ." That's so important on this journey to healing.

Confession changes behavior. That's what God desires for us: to become more and more like Jesus. God offers us forgiveness and mercy. At Calvary, that's what we received. Mercy was so great that grace was free! We were lost, but we have been found by God's compelling love. People know John 3:16, but the next verse says that Jesus didn't come to condemn but to save. He doesn't shame us; he wants to free us. The life God invites us into is unmerited favor, walking in the light! This love was initiated by God, consummated by Jesus, demonstrated by God's grace, perpetuated by God's mercy; and we just say, "Thank you, Jesus," and live a healthy life in response to that. We confess our sins and struggles because it releases us from believing that we are anything less than fragile human beings. We receive it, but let's not ever forget that we need it!

I was at a conference where a speaker was talking about leading in church. He said, "If you have any worship responsibility in a service—lights, music, sound, temperature, all the things that can go wrong in a worship service—when you are in one of those moments, I want you to remember to tell yourself that *There is nobody in here who needs God's love and forgiveness more than I do.* Focus on Jesus instead of what's going wrong in the service today." He was talking to a roomful of preachers. He challenged us to stand up to preach, confessing that nobody in our churches needs God's forgiveness and love more than we do. Particularly for leaders, we fear being "found out." We stuff down our feelings to put on a persona. Inside, we're saying, *I'm not perfect, I don't always have it all together. I may have experienced a failure.* Not being authentic can cause us to go into personal shame: *I'm not good enough. Who am I kidding, pretending I have anything to say about God or what God has done in my life?*

We defeat ourselves. In order to stop defeating ourselves, we have to stop deceiving ourselves. Then we stop the cycle of deceiving others. We perpetuate a shiny version of ourselves, but we need to be open about our worry, bitterness, guilt, anxiety, fear, and insecurity. We're defeated by these things. We have to speak truth to ourselves and to God. The more we do that, the more we are able to speak truth to others—because we've known and experienced the forgiveness of God. We can learn from King David, who learned that confession is the only way to let go of our shame. When we can speak out loud what is really going on with us—the good, the bad, and the ugly—then we can begin to see the light and feel the freedom that Jesus intends for us.

Take some time now in confession. You might want to journal or just talk to God about the true state of your heart. Confess your struggles, confess your doubts, confess your needs, confess your sins, confess your dependence upon God. I promise you that God is faithful and will free you and forgive you. God is at the ready to walk with you through your soul reset. God longs for your wholeness and promises grace and mercy every step of the way. If you are in need of a soul reset, I invite you to take that first step. Ask God to reorder your life and show you once again what it means to live freely and lightly.

Reflection Questions

1. *What do you think it means to "live in the light"?*
2. *Read John 3:17 again. What does it mean to you that God does not condemn you? Do you think people generally think of God as grace-filled or as condemning, and why?*
3. *When something as tragic as suicide happens in a community, what is the faithful response from friends and the faith community? How can you bring light into a tragedy like that?*
4. *How often do you practice confession as part of your spiritual life? Do you go to God often in confession? Do you confess to a small group? Why is confession so important to a life lived in the light? How can confession help you release your shame?*
5. *Here at the end of the last chapter of this book, what is stirred up in your spirit about your need for a soul reset? What do you need to lay down or take up? How is it with your soul? What spiritual practices will you need to intentionally seek a soul reset?*

⏻ The daily spiritual practice for this week is **Confession**. Turn to page 124 to discover ways to practice confession every day in the coming week.

EPILOGUE

I hope this book has inspired you to do a soul reset. This means you are ready to claim the holistic salvation—soul, mind, spirit, body, relationships—that Jesus offers every believer. Resets are necessary to clear the clutter and to operate the way we were created and designed by God. They offer us a fresh start and provide definitive times to begin living from a new perspective. The decision to do a soul reset is not something we do only once in our lives. The journey to wholeness is never complete until we die and go to heaven. This is what it means to be "perfected in love." I am a work in progress. I never would have imagined that the progress I had made following my breakdown would be severely threatened by the tremendous grief I experienced later, in 2012. But I thank God for the continuing journey and that my capacity to live a healthy and whole life continues to grow. I don't run from problems because every challenge is an opportunity to learn new things that help deepen my faith.

I am discovering more things about my soul reset. I have become increasingly aware of my emotional triggers. Triggers are events, circumstances, people, or situations that may stir an emotional reaction inside of us. The very process of writing this book and recalling the details of my story was a trigger for me. There were days after a writing session when I simply wanted to go home and get in the bed. I felt drained and like I was reliving the depression, shame, and grief. The feelings were so real and raw. Instead, I shared what I was feeling in prayer, and I practiced the very things I write about in this book. Being aware of your triggers is a way to empower yourself to act quickly to avoid the habits that lead to depression, shame, exhaustion, or burnout. I know how easy it would be for me to revert to isolation and bad habits. So, a trigger now reminds me to spend more time with God. I am acutely aware of the need to practice good spiritual habits. They grow my relationship with Jesus, and they help me maintain my center.

A *soul reset* is the pouring out of one's self to God. It means laying yourself at the altar and earnestly seeking God's face. It means a season of fervent praying and fasting. It includes finding new and meaningful ways to connect with Jesus, the lover of our souls. I have recently discovered the joy of playing the piano. Music feeds my soul. I worship God in my playing, and the joy I experience is indescribable. I am discovering new ways to express myself. Playing the piano releases my creativity. It also helps me stay disciplined in other areas of my life. The process of regular practice, learning new songs, and studying are quite helpful in my ministry. Don't be surprised if your reset leads to a new discovery for you and unexpected ways to express your love for Jesus.

The ultimate goal of a soul reset is to live our best lives now, to experience the abundant life that Jesus promised us. Sometimes this means fighting for joy in the midst of difficult situations. The apostle Paul was in prison, getting ready to be executed, and he penned a letter to the church in Philippi about joy. He told them to "always be full of joy in the Lord. I say it again—rejoice!" (Phil. 4:4, NLT). It is not easy, but it is possible, especially when you remember that in God's presence is fullness of joy! That is why these spiritual practices are so important and vital for our discipleship journey. They are not about being a better church member. They are not about being a perfect leader. They are not about having the appearance of religiosity or holiness. They are about growing in our relationship with God and staying in love with Jesus.

This is the foundation for healthy and whole living. It is the foundation for creating a healthy faith community. Each passing day teaches me that if I stay connected to Jesus and grounded in my faith, then no matter what I face, it doesn't have to overwhelm me. I am learning that no matter what I go through, I am not going through it alone. Remember,

> "When you pass through deep waters, I will be with you;
> your troubles will not overwhelm you.
> When you pass through fire, you will not be burned,
> the hard trials that come will not hurt you.
> For I am the LORD your God!" (Isa. 43:2, GNT)

My prayer is that your soul reset will set a new course for your life. I believe that it will change the way you lead yourself and others. As a result, your church, your family, and your workplace will never ever be the same again. In Jesus' name! Amen.

DAILY SPIRITUAL PRACTICES
FOR A SOUL RESET

WEEK

1

The Practice of *Examen*

The Prayer of Examen is a spiritual practice introduced by Ignatius of Loyola (1491–1556 CE) that invites a deep inward reflection on each day as an exercise in noticing the movement of God, our connectedness to God throughout the day, and learning to discern the will of God. In the practice of *examen*, we seek and find God in all things of daily life. As we examine each day, we look for those moments when we felt close to God, which Ignatius describes as *consolation*. We then look for those moments in which we felt disconnected from God, defined by Ignatius as *desolation*. In both spaces, we can seek God and hear from God about God's will for us, discover the truth about who we are, and be reminded that we are ever held by a good and loving God.

This week, you are invited to close each day with the practice of *examen*. Find a quiet place, and turn off your phone and any other distractions. Light a candle and invite God to be present with you. Take some deep breaths, and settle into your body and into the quiet. Begin each practice by reviewing the day in your mind, paying attention to moments of joy, moments of confusion, moments of sadness, or moments of peace. Daily prompts for each day are listed below.

Day 1: *What brought you the most joy today? Give thanks to God. When did you feel most connected to God? Give thanks to God. Did you feel sad today? Share your raw and unabridged feelings with God. Then, sit in silence and listen for God's voice reminding you that you are loved and held in grace.*

Day 2: *If you could relive a moment from today, which would it be? Where was God in this wonderful moment? What did you experience or discover about the love and grace of God today?*

Day 3: *Jesus invites us to live lightly and freely with him each day. Did you feel light and free today? If yes, what was it like to walk unburdened through the day? If no, what is needed to accept Jesus' invitation to a light and free kind of living? Listen to God in the silence of your heart about what is keeping you from freedom.*

Day 4: *Reflect on your ability to give and receive love today. Was love easy or difficult to give away? Was love easy or difficult to receive? Look for God in these moments of giving and receiving love today, and ask God to teach you more about God's generous ways of loving.*

Day 5: *Rehearse the day in your mind, pausing at each moment of gratitude to give thanks. Invite God to reset your heart, to clear away the clutter of guilt, harsh words, words left unsaid, actions taken or left undone. Let God's grace wash over the desolation and guide you to a place of consolation where you can always begin again.*

Day 6: *How is it with your soul? Listen to your body, to your feelings, and to your thoughts. Share with God how your soul is doing today. Then, listen for God's voice to speak to your heart.*

Day 7: *Reflect on the idea of wholeness. What images come to your mind? Do you feel whole? If not, what is keeping you from wholeness? If yes, how did you come to be whole, and what does it feel like? Give thanks for where you are right now on the journey and invite God to speak to your heart in the quiet.*

WEEK 2

The Practice of Prayer

The practice of prayer simply means to spend time with God. Sometimes we talk; sometimes we listen; sometimes we seek; sometimes we rest—all are actions of practicing prayer. Throughout the scriptures, we have examples of varying forms of prayer, from Abraham stargazing with God; to David worshiping, lamenting, and grieving, and then praising God again; to Elijah in a cave listening for God; to Jesus himself giving us the words to pray. The Bible shows us time and again that God desires time and conversation with us.

This week, you will be invited into various forms of prayer, with the simple task of sitting with God. Set aside a period of time each day and designate a place that will be devoted to your prayer practice. Make this an intentional, set-apart time just for you and God to spend some time together.

Day 1: *Settle into a quiet space, and turn off your phone. Sit for a moment in silence, and center your thoughts and your heart on drawing near to God. Once you are settled, set an intention of simply sitting in the presence of God. When tasks or worries or even fears come into your mind, acknowledge them before God, and ask God to hold them in God's hands. Pay attention to what messages God might have for you—words to bring you comfort or encouragement or maybe even just a feeling of peace or mercy. This practice of prayer requires no words or striving; this is simply a time for you to sit with God and to let your thoughts and feelings come and go. When you are ready, end your prayer time by praying The Lord's Prayer.*

Day 2: *For your prayer practice today, you are invited to write a letter to God. Consider that God invites us into friendship. Friends have regular conversations, sharing hopes and fears, dreams and tri-als. Sit down with a piece of paper and a pen today, and write a letter to God, your friend. Share all that is going on in your life right now, what is on your mind, what is going on with your family, what you are struggling with, what you are grateful for—everything that you would share with your very best friend.*

Day 3: *Today, you are invited to make* silence *your friend. Set aside some time to block out any noise and create an opportunity to listen for the still, small voice of a loving God. Let your thoughts float away like clouds, and let the silence clear your heart and mind. Don't strive or try to achieve in these moments. Simply sit in God's presence and be still.*

Day 4: *Sometimes life comes at us, and before we know it, our hearts are overcome with worry, fear, and anxious thoughts. Trials and suffering can make us feel like there is nothing good about our* lives or that we'll never experience joy again. The Psalms teach us how to praise God, even in our suffering. David lays out all his feelings before God—anger, uncertainty, fear, defeat, sadness, depression—but he circles back to his love for God and finds a way to "yet praise," even when he faces trials. Name before God your fears and worries, your trials and anxious thoughts. Then, close your prayer with words of praise, and set your heart to praise.

Day 5: *Practice prayer today by looking for God everywhere. Keep your eyes and ears open to notice the beauty of creation, encouraging words from a friend, the wind blowing across your face. Notice the goodness of God all around you, and get caught up in it. Set your heart on seeking God, on looking for God's movement and listening for God's voice all day long.*

Day 6: *Today, align your prayer with your breath by practicing a breath prayer. Throughout the day, as often as you can, let your heart whisper as you inhale, "Lord Jesus Christ"; and as you exhale, "have mercy on me, a sinner."*

Day 7: *How is it with your soul right now? Ask God to reveal the places in your life that are thriving, and then ask God to show you the places that need new life. Pray for a clean heart and a renewed spirit.*

WEEK

3

The Practice of Fasting

Fasting can be difficult to understand and to practice. Sometimes it can get misconstrued and confused with dieting, but it has nothing to do with weight loss. Fasting is about self-denial, about saying yes to God by saying no to some other competing desire. This week, you'll do a daily fast from various things that compete for space in your heart and mind, reminding you of your true desire to give God your whole heart.

Day 1: *Fast from social media for twenty-four hours. Turn these apps off on your phone, and do your best not to go there on your computer. Notice any impulses you have to check your phone or the way you get on your computer and begin to type "Facebook" before you even realize it. As you sense those impulses, ask God to be the Lord of your life. Ask God for help to make social media a fun, "extra" thing in your life and not a distraction that keeps you from being fully present with God and with your friends and family.*

Day 2: *Fast from food from sundown to sundown. During your last meal, ask God to be your strength as you sleep and go about your day, relying only on God. Be sure to drink plenty of water. Throughout your fasting day, notice your cravings, your stamina, and your clarity. Lean on God's strength, and ask God to help you depend on God each and every day. When you sit down to eat again, give thanks to God for God's strength in you and God's presence with you always.*

Day 3: *Fast from words. As much as possible, refrain from speaking for a period of time. You may need to share your practice with family or coworkers ahead of time. This is a practice of being slow to speak and quick to listen. Pay attention to what you hear when you're not forming your own responses constantly.*

Day 4: *Fast from using plastic. As best you can, refrain from using any quick-and-easy, throwaway products. Notice the extra effort of washing a glass or carrying around a reusable water bottle. Pay attention to what you throw away in a day, and consider how you could cut back on waste by making a few intentional choices.*

Day 5: *Fast from excess. Super-sizing and going back for second helpings, retail therapy, and stockpiling can be second nature for many of us. Spend twenty-four hours practicing simplicity and moderation. Avoid second helpings. Don't buy anything that you don't need. Spend some time in your closet, purging unnecessary items and donating them to a thrift store. Spend this day taking only what you need from it and nothing more. Notice how it feels to deny yourself something that you want. Ask God to teach you to live simply and to depend on God.*

Day 6: *Fast from complaining and criticism. Take on a spirit of gentleness and encouragement for a day. What happens to your mood? to your countenance?*

Day 7: *Fast from technology. Go for a walk, take a nap, write letters, cook a great meal. Let your eyes look at real things right in front of you, and be present where you are.*

WEEK

4

The Practice of Taking Care of Your Body

Sometimes we think of our spiritual practices and life with God as separate from how we treat our bodies. But we are whole persons, created by God—body, mind, and spirit. God's desire for our wholeness is not only about our hearts but also about our whole selves. This week, we will seek wholeness by taking care of our bodies.

Day 1: *Sleep eight hours. Look at your schedule for the week and make a plan to get eight full hours of sleep each night this week. As you go to sleep each night, ask God to bring you rest. Pay attention to the way your rested body serves you throughout the day. How does rest equip you for the challenges of each day? How does rest allow for deeper connection to God?*

Day 2: *Drink plenty of water. Over the course of the day, be intentional about drinking eight large glasses of water. With each glass, reflect on Jesus as the source of Living Water that sustains you for a life with God. Notice how hydrating makes you feel—are you more energized? Are you more confident, knowing you are making good choices for your health?*

Day 3: *Go for a long walk if you are able, soaking up the sun and taking deep breaths. Let endorphins kick in, and feel the strength of your legs to carry you. Feel your back straighten as you take long strides. With every breath, breathe in the grace of God; as you exhale, breathe out your praise to God.*

Day 4: *Fast from sugar. Most of us have no idea how much sugar we take in each day. Spend the day taking care of your body by relentlessly avoiding sugar. Say no to the sugary coffee creamer or the honey in your tea. Say no to the office snack drawer or the plate of cupcakes that showed up without warning. Say no to the soda that you've thought you had to have at 3:00 p.m. every day. Notice how many ways sugar infiltrates your day without your even knowing it. After today, determine which forms of sugar you could permanently cut from your routine to take better care of your body.*

Day 5: *Today, write a letter thanking your body for what it does for you. God made our bodies in such an awesome way and for incredible things. Consider all that your body does for you. Give thanks for it, and consider how you might take better care of your body as an act of worship to the God who created you.*

Day 6: *Find a workout buddy. Who will be your accountability partner as you set out to take good care of your body? Make that your number-one task today.*

Day 7: *Cook your favorite healthy meal, and have dinner with your friends and family. Fuel your body with healthy food, and fuel your spirit with intentional time with loved ones, gathered at the table. Pray a blessing over your meal and over your friends.*

WEEK

5

The Practice of Worship

Worship is more than simply a one-hour experience, one day a week. Worship is a lifestyle. Worship is acknowledging that God is God and we are not. We worship because God is holy. We worship because God's faithfulness demands a response. We worship because spending time with God makes us whole. Worship can mean everything from lament to adoration, and we can be sure that God can handle however we come to worship.

Day 1: *Before you get to worship this week, spend some time considering the practice of lament. Lament is a biblical and holy practice of grieving before God, telling God exactly how we feel about what is happening in our lives, and then pleading with God to come near. The Psalms show us this pattern over and over. Psalmists write in their despair, naming their true feelings to God but always circling back to a word of worship or invitation for God to come near. Read*

Psalm 22, and note the words of lament and the words of worship. Rewrite the psalm in your own words. What in your own life or in the world right now causes you to lament?

Day 2: *Reflect on your feelings about lament. Are you free to bring all your thoughts and feelings to God, no matter what they are? Do you trust that God loves you, regardless of your raw emotions? Write a psalm of lament over a source of grief or despair in your own life. Trust that God can handle your deepest feelings.*

Day 3: *Choose a worship song or hymn that will be your theme for the day. Listen to the song over and over throughout the day, lifting your heart to God in worship each time you hear it. Reflect on the ways in which having an attitude of worship affects your day.*

Day 4: *Adore God today. Look for God's majesty all around you, in creation and in others. Speak your praises to God audibly or in your heart as they rise up within you. Thank God for all that God has brought you through. At the end of the day, review all the ways you noticed God, and give thanks.*

Day 5: *Practice corporate worship. Be intentional as you prepare for church this week. Walk in to worship with an attitude of expectation to encounter the living God. Let your praises rise to God, and expect that God's Spirit will inhabit the praises of God's people.*

Day 6: *What do you love to do—like, really, really love to do? Play an instrument? Sing? Play a sport? Balance spreadsheets? Paint or take photos? Give thanks to God for that passion, and spend some time with God as you practice or perform your hobby. Let a spirit of worship rise up within you as you do the thing you love to do and give glory to God.*

Day 7: *Subscribe to a worship podcast—your favorite Christian author, pastor, singer, or a podcast of a liturgy. Make a point to listen to the podcast on one of your car trips during the day, and let worship be part of your everyday activity.*

WEEK

6

The Practice of Confession

A key element of the journey to wholeness is authenticity or vulnerability. When we are seeking wholeness, we drop any pretense and take the brave, vulnerable step toward authenticity. The practice we'll focus on this week is confession. Instead of different daily exercises, you're invited to write a prayer of confession at the end of each day this week. Be vulnerable with God about when you lost your temper or were impatient with someone that day. Note when you felt yourself hiding behind a shinier version of yourself instead of letting your true self show through, and confess that too. The practice of being honest with ourselves and honest with God propels us on our soul reset journey.

ABOUT THE AUTHOR

A nationally recognized leader, speaker, and author on evangelism and church revitalization, the Rev. Junius B. Dotson is the General Secretary (CEO) of Discipleship Ministries. Dotson launched "See All the People," the highly successful churchwide initiative that helps church leaders concentrate on intentional discipleship, while learning new behaviors around engaging their surrounding community. This initiative currently includes his ninety-second daily radio series *See All the People*, which is featured on more than forty radio stations across the United States.

Rev. Dotson is the author of *Developing an Intentional Discipleship System: A Guide for Congregations* and *Engaging Your Community: A Guide to Seeing All the People*. Both resources help congregations look beyond their walls, acknowledging that God calls us to have "meaningful relationships in authentic, organic and consistent ways."

As a leader who responds to challenges and opportunities in new and creative ways, Rev. Dotson believes that effective ministry is about training, developing, and empowering leaders to establish ministries that address the needs of the whole person—body, mind, and spirit.

Prior to his present position, Rev. Dotson was senior pastor of Saint Mark United Methodist Church in Wichita, Kansas, where he was instrumental in transforming the 3,500-member church into a multicampus congregation.

Rev. Dotson received his undergraduate degree in political science, with a concentration in economics, at the University of Texas at Arlington. While attending UT-Arlington, he was president of the local chapter of Alpha Phi Alpha, the nation's oldest African-American fraternity. Rev. Dotson began his graduate work at Perkins School of Theology at Southern Methodist University and earned his Master of Divinity degree from the Pacific School of Religion in Berkeley, California. He was ordained in June 1992.

In 1996, Rev. Dotson responded to the challenge of planting Genesis United Methodist Church, a new and innovative church in the Silicon Valley of California, which grew into a diverse faith community of nearly 500 people.

Junius is a native of Houston, Texas. He is the proud father of two adult children, Wesley and Janelle. He is an avid Dallas Cowboys fan and enjoys playing the piano.

Use *Soul Reset* as a churchwide worship experience

Experience *Soul Reset* at any age with these companion products for pastors, adults, children, and youth.

Companion Resources include

Participant's Book...........................978-0-8358-1896-4........$14.99
DVD...978-0-8358-1900-8.......$29.99
Adult Group Guide PDF................978-0-8358-1901-5..........$9.99
Youth Group Guide PDF................978-0-8358-1902-2..........$9.99
Children's Group Guide Guide PDF.......978-0-8358-1903-9..........$9.99
Sermon Starters PDF.....................978-0-8358-1904-6..........$9.99
eCourse..........................UReLearning.UpperRoom.org........$19.00

Visit **SoulReset.org** to learn more.